Debts of the State and the Danger of Economic Collapse

Debts of the State and the Danger of Economic Collapse

Ivan Ovcaricek-Rostok

Strategic Book Publishing and Rights Co.

Strategic Book Publishing and Rights Co.
12620 FM 1960, Suite A4-507
Houston, TX 77065
www.sbpra.com

For information about special discounts for bulk purchases, please contact Strategic Book Publishing and Rights Co. Special Sales, at bookorder@sbpra.net.

ISBN: 978-1-63135-243-0

It's a sin to leave debts to children.
  Debts are bad for children.

—Dr. sc. Ivan Ovcaricek-Rostok

ACKNOWLEDGMENT

I thank the friends from the SBPRA who were included in the publication of this book and were very helpful, especially Mrs. Katie Smith, and Mr. Bruce Martin. I also thank Mr Hari, Mr Tom Wallace, Mrs Lynn Eddy, Mrs Ellen Green, Mrs Deanna, and Mrs Tara Jay.

Table of Contents

PREFACE

Today, in about fifty countries around the world, there exists an excessive amount of debt. This debt grows from year to year and is a major economic problem. The problem is even greater because it rests in the most developed countries in the world—the United States, the United Kingdom, Germany, France, Italy, and Japan, to name a few. By 2013, this debt became so great that it threatened to cause a global economic collapse. Incurring further debts must be stopped and we must begin to gradually decrease the existing ones.

The problem is even more difficult because some countries have entered a state of eternal debt. Most notable is the United States, which holds about one-quarter of the world economy. It would take over 100 years of a high growth rate to pay off the current debt by an increase in the gross domestic product. Paying it off will only be possible by the quick introduction of a combination of the principle of economic duals and the category of diversified money. This concept was described in detail in my earlier work, *The Economic Success of the State: The Principle of Economic Duals and the Category of Diversified Money*.

The beginning of the economic collapse will likely begin when, for the first time, credit is not approved to cover the large budget deficits in the U.S. or the UK. This illiquidity will then enter the world economic system and begin to spread uncontrollably, infecting every country with this economic disease. The consequence will be a reduction in the volume of world production. Correcting this deviation will require up to ten years. The economic collapse could cause serious global political devastation that could be very encumbering. This would also put a large part of the rights and benefits the people of the world enjoy into question. The world's political leaders need to take these warning signs seriously. Measures should have begun about five years ago to cut down expenses and reduce spending to realistic levels.

The situation now is that even months of waiting can cause big problems. In particular, the leaders in the U.S. and UK should be warned of the serious situation. Their two countries are approaching a summative debt that is equal to the size of one-half of the total debts of the rest of the world. It is also evident that the huge benefits of such economies benefit a very narrow section of the world's population. It increases the stratification of society in the most developed countries. At one end there is fabulous luxury, and at the other are people struggling for the most basic needs. You do not need to advocate the communist formula of "From each according to his ability, to each according to his needs," but neither can we condone gaining huge profits gained through the conceptual errors of state policy.

This text is an in-depth expansion of the text in *The Economic Success of the State: The Principle of Economic Duals and the Category of Diversified Money.* Parts of this book were in my earlier text and have been used in both original and revised forms. This is because the problems are entwined. It was not possible to deal with one problem without treating the other that is inseparably connected with it.

The Problem for the U.S.

Because of the conceptual deficiencies in free international trade, the United States fell into huge international debt and in the parallel state of deviations of eternal debt and credit inversion. This could lead the country to an economic collapse that would last for many years. If this happens, the entire global economy will suffer an uncontrollable economic collapse with consequences much worse than the one that lasted from 1929–33.

For this reason, the U.S. must be a leader in finding the way out of the current difficult economic situation. According to recent estimates, even with the best effort, the economic disease will last about ten years. It will be necessary to reconstruct and improve the economic systems of the U.S. and the European Union. The most developed countries will have to move to an economic model where they spend no more than their domestic products produce. Anything else is an economic deviation.

INTRODUCTION

The Concept and Goals of the Research

The economies of several of the most developed countries in the world have entered large debts because of two main factors: foreign trade and state budget deficits. These debts are steadily increasing. The indebted states have no concept of how to get out of this situation. These governments need to solve a few fundamental problems:

- How to stop going further into debt
- How to begin to amortize the accumulated debt
- How to form government policies that will prevent a large-scale economic collapse

This study has several objectives:

- To explain the conceptual framework for the amortization of debts and their reduction within an economically realistic framework
- To explain the concepts of economic deviations, credit inversions, and conditions of eternal debt
- To explain the dangers of an economic collapse
- To lay out a possible framework for the transformation of the current economic situation into an improved one

Research Methods

To get relevant results, several appropriate research methods were used, including analysis and synthesis, generalization and specialization, induction and deduction, and modeling.

The Actuality of the Theme

The theme of this research is very actual. The most developed states will not be able to simply wiggle their way out of their over indebtedness for one primary reason—a lack of production. They go into debt for consumption, and that is a conceptual error. After a careful reading of this work, it will be quickly realized where the deviation of such a policy is. It will probably be most accurately observed in the United State. If the U.S. had more insight into the problem of indebtedness, they could have prevented the economic deviation that caused the loss of over $17.5 billion. The consequences of this will last for years. The relevant details are described in the further text.

The Purpose of the Research

This research was conducted with the intention of pointing out the importance of rational economic policies for states, because it is a complex system. Upon entering an election campaign, the political candidates are involved in drawing up electoral programs, the main part of which deals with problems in economic policy. For this reason, the economic premises of this study are shown as simply as possible to be useful to those who are not professional economists.

Basis for the Research

In this study, various data sources are used as a base. Most of them are related to the United States. The reason for this is that the U.S. is the most developed economic country in the world. Whatever happens economically in the U.S. reflects on the rest of the world. In addition to the U.S., data for the UK, Croatia, and forty-seven other countries have been used.

Chapter 1

Problems of Debt

1. The Economic System and Debt

The modern economic system of each country consists of five basic elements: the production of economic goods, the supply of economic goods, the demand of economic goods, stable money, and a regulated market for trading economic goods. If any of these elements does not fulfil its function, the results are anomalies in the economic system. A healthy economy needs all five elements to be active.

The supply of economic goods is a result of their production, and the demand for those goods is a result of the buying power of customers. Money is the general equivalent value of material goods. A regulated market means there are codified rules of conduct in the supply and demand of economic goods. The processing of elements in the economic system takes place in an economic space and within real time. The economic system of each country has its own specifics for organizing the economic elements.

The only universal element in the economic system is money. Through it, three basic functions are realized—the payment of obligations arising from the base of processing economic elements, calculations of economic processing, and the storage of economic results achieved in the economic processing. In a formed economic system the states are also like economic subjects—big ones. The most developed countries in the world run their economic affairs with large deficits. They cover these losses by going into debt in various forms.

Business at the state level is organized by political parties. They are the only ones responsible for the quality of that business.

2. The Problem of the Size of Debt

The debts of a country emerge from within political parties. There are two main types of these programs. The first are those that advocate the interests of assets and property in the state, and the other is those who advocate the interests of labor. Out of this logic, two main types of government debt are generated. One type of debt is caused by foreign trade and other from the business of the state budget. The debts of foreign trade are generated by the economic subjects of the state and the population. They arise because of an imbalance in the trade import and export of economic resources. State budget debts are generated by the government and occur because of an imbalance of the revenue and expenditures of the state.

Debts of foreign trade are causally and consequentially associated with the foreign policy of the state. Debts of an entrepreneurial nature have a retroactive economic effect. This means that they can be directly depreciated by the production of material goods and services. The debts of the state budget, with some minor exceptions, have no direct retroactive economic effect. They cannot be amortized on this basis. They are amortized from the state budget expenditures.

Today, the most developed states are deeply in debt because of foreign trade, and a smaller number of lower developed states are their creditors. This is an economic deviation produced by the policies of the most developed countries. In addition, the most developed countries have large internal and external debts in the state budgets. If we summarize both situations, it is easy to see the high level of indebtedness, which is a threat to world economic stability because the distribution of the global economic potential is mainly allocated in two large complex economic spaces—the U.S. and the EU. These two economic spaces hold about forty-seven percent of the world's economy.

3. The Problem of the Dynamics of Debt

Amortization of a country's debts is not a simple question. It is politically very sensitive. Politicians often live their professional lives on promises regarding the consumption and spending of what has not yet been produced and not the result of normal economic processing. Economically educated people expect economically optimal decisions to be issued. The economics of states is, figuratively speaking, a big lever with two equal legs, which always have to be in horizontal position. On one of its sides are value receipts and on the other value expenditures. Uncontrolled adding of burden on one of these sides causes inbalance and destabilization. Economically educated people know this. Economically, not enough educated people are not aware of it. Each of the sides of this lever is also a network made up of chains and millions of links. Interventions in this system must not be unreasonable. It is like the nervous system of humans. First you need to take into account not to disturb the balance of the "lever," and secondly, that the "chains" in the network do not break. However, economic laws are inexorable. You can spend only what you produce. Spending on debt brings harm in the long run because the credit has two phases. The first shorter phase is when the credit is obtained and when you get the desired goods to use them. A feeling of enthusiasm and satisfaction then occurs. The second phase is longer, when the debt has to be repaid. That brings on a feeling of discomfort and depression.

The repayment, or amortization, of debt for an over-indebted state should have three phases:

- Stopping the successive growth of debt.
- Stabilizing the economic equilibrium.
- Reducing the debt.

3.1 Stopping the Successive Growth of Debt

For many years, the debts of developed countries have characteristically had steady growth. This is an economic negative tendency. As an example, one can look at the growth of debt arising from the foreign trade of the United States and Croatia.

Table 1: Movement of Total External Debt of the U.S. and Croatia

Year	Amount of the external debt USA {in millions of dollars}	Index	Amount of the external debt Croatia {in millions of euros}	Index
2003	6,946,289	100	18,727	100
2004	8,353,479	120	22,933	122
2005	9,476,403	136	25,761	138

Year	Amount of the external debt USA {in millions of dollars}	Index	Amount of the external debt Croatia {in millions of euros}	Index
2006	11,204,108	161	29,273	156
2007	13,427,103	193	32,929	176
2008	13,749,570	198	39,124	209
2009	13,767,867	198	43,117	230
2010	14,456,194	208	45,860	249

In the first phase, the growth of state debts should be stopped at current levels. At this stage a program of economic balance should be made and realized. A balance of foreign trade exports and imports should be established, and the income and expenditures of state budgets should be realized. The establishment of these balances is a difficult task because it has a huge impact on the internal and external policies, economic development, and the state's purchasing power. With such a program, all the direct economic consequences for the country should be identified and collateral damage assessed. If such a phase is not carried out, a future financial collapse of the state is inevitable.

3.2 Stabilizing the Economic Equilibrium

When a program of the interruption of the successive growth of debt is executed, its stabilization should start. Here, the political parties must play the most important role, especially those that are ruling. As noted earlier, voters at elections are attracted by the promise of the possibility of spending and living at the expense of the state. This applies in particular to various government grants, steady growth in wages (regardless of productivity), expansion of benefits from the work, the extension of health care without limitation, extending the right of education for occupations that do not guarantee the possibility of employment, and earlier retirement without economic criteria. Therefore, political parties should be a source of rationalism. They should not propagate the illusion of the economic omnipotence of the state. They must practice a policy of economic stabilization, and within that, the economic balance of the country.

3.3 Reduction of Debts

The program to reduce state debts should contain two things—the reduction of the foreign trade deficit and the balancing of the state budget. There are two main options. The first is to introduce the application of diversified money, and the second is the principle of economic duals. Foreign trade and the national budget are the state's two largest economic complexes. They determine the economic success of the country. By introducing the function of diversified money, the imbalance of foreign trade is eliminated. By applying the principle of economic duals, the level of economic activity is upgraded, thus creating financial effects for the repayment of the debts of the state budget without the need for broadening the tax base.

Chapter 2

Amortization of Debts

4. The Amortization Schedule

The debt of the state budget is subject to the obligation of depreciation or the return of the borrowed money. Because the government debt has no financial effect if returned, it is a clear burden for the state. Its depreciation is possible in several ways:

- Increasing the tax burden
- Changes in the structure of expenditures so that some expenses are reduced or abolished and put toward debt repayment instead
- By the sale of state assets

Deviation budget expenditures are created by the political parties in power by the realization of their electoral programs. In these programs, a lack of knowledge about the economics of the state and political manipulation can be seen. Because of this, it is very important to eliminate the reasons for poor political decisions. In their election proposals, politicians do not accurately calculate the resulting economic impact of those programs.

5. Amortization of Debts in Foreign Trade

The only economic solution for balancing the foreign trade deficit is the introduction of diversified money. This is an economic means of rationalization of state economics. International trade is needed because no country can produce all the goods and services it needs. Besides, this trade is useful for the country's trading partners. However, in these transactions a trading deficit usually occurs for one of the countries involved.

The subject of this analysis will be a deficit from an economic deviation. In order to stimulate exports to maintain the level of domestic production, the exporting countries are willing to finance the countries that buy their products. The subject for consideration in this analysis will be the problems that can occur in the importing countries.

In order for Country A to buy as many goods as possible from Country B, Country B gladly grants credit to Country A at relatively favorable terms. This means that Country A will go into debt today and buy the goods that it will pay for tomorrow. If Country A accepts the credit, it probably has anticipated the financial construction to repay the loan. That plan is probably based on the supposition that Country A will be able to increase its exports to Country B in the future, and use those exports to repay the debt. The goods purchased on credit by Country A will be more expensive because of the amount of interest that it will pay to Country B for the period of the loan.

Such an arrangement generally does not take into consideration the possibility of future changes that could prevent the repaying of the loan by exports. However, if these changes do occur it could cause damage to Country A. Other circumstances may occur that prevent the realization of the repayment of the debt. As a result, the repayment period could be significantly extended. Suppose that in this case the repayment period of one year is extended to five years, and that the interest rate is increased from two percent to six percent per annum. The purchased goods then become twenty percent more expensive. The initial benefit of the import of goods is then annulled or even turned into a detriment. This is a credit inversion.

The import on credit is a potential risk for the country as well as for the consumers. This could also be the reason for an increase in the external debt of Country A, as often occurs in many countries, and then it becomes a problem for the world economy. Such events are economic deviations. Because of possible changes in circumstances and conditions of going into debt with foreign countries, the application of a general economic principle is required. Country A must maintain the balance of exports and imports with Country B. This is often not respected, and it is always the fault of the state's policy because it causes the economic deviations for its own interests and goals.

The question is how to achieve the trade balance in individual countries. The nature of interstate economic relations is such that the so-called gravity economic relationships between states are structurally different. The consequences of trade imbalances are also different, and any imbalance can cause an economic deviation. Some of them eliminate each other on a macro level, which reduces the global economic deviation. A good example for this is Croatia and the U.S. Their exports and imports are especially imbalanced with several countries. This is illustrated in Tables 2 and 3.

Table 2: Croatian Exports and Imports in 2008 (in thousands of dollars)

Mark	Country	Export	Import	Coverage of import in %
01	Austria	815.658	1,509.195	54.0
02	Belgium	88.836	310.656	28.6
03	Czech	148.097	631.313	23.5
04	France	297.548	1,000.572	29.7
05	Italy	2,694.137	5,258.688	51.2
06	Germany	1,518.133	4,115.890	36.9
07	Russia	186.208	3,200.867	5.8
08	Japan	60.800	439.566	13.8
09	China	36.254	1,885.833	1.9
10	Turkey	88.315	477.033	18.5
11	Morocco	10.590	132.729	8.0
12	USA	350.228	625.474	56.0
	Total	**6,294.804**	**19,587.816**	**32.1**

Table 3: U.S. Exports and Imports in 2005 (in billions of dollars)

Mark	Country	Export	Import	Coverage of import in %
01	Canada	211.9	290.4	73.0
02	Mexico	120.4	170.1	70.8
03	Japan	55.5	138.0	40.2
04	China	41.9	243.5	17.2

Mark	Country	Export	Import	Coverage of import in %
05	UK	38.6	51.0	75.7
06	Germany	34.2	84.8	40.3
07	South Korea	27.8	43.8	63.4
08	Netherlands	26.5	0.0	***
09	France	22.4	33.8	66.2
10	Taiwan	22.1	34.8	63.5
	Total	**601.3**	**1,090.2**	**55.2**

There is an even more serious problem if the movement of the total foreign debt of Croatia is added to the previous imbalance with several other countries.

Table 4: Movement of Total External Debt in Croatia (in millions of euros)

Year	Amount of foreign debt	Index
2003	18.727	100
2004	22.933	122
2005	25.761	138
2006	29.273	156
2007	32.929	176
2998	39.124	209
2009	43.117	230
2010	45.860	249

From the data in Table 4, it can be seen that the Croatian foreign debt is constantly growing at a relatively high rate. Therefore, it is an economic necessity that Croatia establish an economic balance of foreign trade. The same applies to the U.S. The balance can be achieved by organizing supplements to the financial system.

5.1 The Effect of Diversified Money in the Repayment of Foreign Trade Debts

The economic solution for fixing the balance of foreign trade should be the introduction of diversified money. It is the economic means to rationalize the economics of the state. Because each import is normally paid in advance, a special kind of money for imports from each country should be established. The quantity would be limited according to the volume of the export. Interstate trade is a necessity because each country cannot, or is not interested in, producing all the goods that it consumes. Furthermore, the trade is useful for the country's commercial partners. In the case where a trade deficit occurs in one of the countries involved, that money would be limited by the export volume. With this money, the import for Country A would be economically limited, and the export into Country B stimulated. This would be the diversified money, and imports could only be paid for with such specialized money.

Those without this type money in a bank transfer account could not import goods. The importer would buy that specialized currency from the bank and have it put in a special account to cover the cost of the intended import. The money would be bought at a diversified exchange rate determined by the banks and based on the supply and demand of such money. This would be applied to all import businesses. For example, in Croatia kunas could be bought to purchase imports from Italy, China, Russia, etc. The category of diversified money refers to internal national domestic money. It's an accounting category and applies only to the foreign trade of a state to another state. Its value is determined on the basis of supply and demand arising from the export and import situation of the country compared to another partner country.

In such a case, imported Chinese goods could not be a value that is fifty-two times greater than the value of the exports to China. For example: in the USA, dollars could be bought to purchase imports from Italy, China, Russia, etc. In such case imported Chinese goods could not be a value that is about six times grater than the value of the export from the USA to China. Therefore, an example is given to show the difference between the general interstate rate of the U.S. currency and the exchange rate, which is applied in the economic area of it for balancing the value of exports and imports.

The existence of diversified money would be economically beneficial for each country that would become a chronic debtor without it. In that case, the comparative advantages of interstate trade through the so-called opportunity costs of production could be used. In the context of diversified money, if the economic scenario for Croatia is analyzed then the current foreign trade deficit and foreign debt could be consolidated two ways. The existing external debt could be paid from the net gains from tourism, or the country could eliminate the deficit in the value of the trade goods in two parts. One would result from a decrease in imports and the other from an increase in exports. Otherwise, Croatia will find itself in eternal debt. In the case of the introduction of diversified money, the balance of the exports and imports of Croatia would be brought into equilibrium. The same applies to the U.S. If the above tables are recalculated, the effects of this could be seen in Tables 5 and 6.

Table 5: Croatian Exports and Imports for 2008 with the Introduction of Diversified Money (in thousands of dollars)

Mark	Country	Export	Import	Coverage of import in %
01	Austria	1,162.426	1,162.426	100
02	Belgium	199.746	199.746	100
03	Czech	389.705	389.705	100
04	France	649.060	649.060	100
05	Italy	3,976.413	3,976.413	100
06	Germany	2,817.012	2,817.012	100
07	Russia	1,693.538	1,693.538	100
08	Japan	250.183	250.183	100
09	China	961.044	961.044	100
10	Turkey	282.674	282.674	100
11	Morocco	71.660	71.660	100
12	USA	487.851	487.851	100
	Total	**12,941.312**	**12,941.312**	**100**

Table 6: U.S. Exports and Imports in 2005 with the Introduction of Diversified Money (in billions of dollars)

Mark	Country	Export	Import	Coverage of import in %
01	Canada	251.2	251.2	100
02	Mexico	145.3	145.3	100
03	Japan	96.8	96.8	100

Mark	Country	Export	Import	Coverage of import in %
04	China	142.7	142.7	100
05	UK	44.8	44.8	100
06	Germany	59.5	59.5	100
07	South Korea	35.8	35.8	100
08	Netherlands	13.3	13.3	100
09	France	28.1	28.1	100
10	Taiwan	28.5	28.5	100
	Total	**846.0**	**846.0**	100

The existence of diversified money would stimulate increased interest in exports, and at the same time it would limit imports. It would have a positive effect on the economy. In the debtor countries, it would automatically contribute to an increase in the rate of the gross domestic product, reduce unemployment, increase state budget revenue, reduce the debt to foreign countries, and increase the country's liquidity, as well as help successfully overcome economic deviations. At the same time, it would not cause inflation or a depreciation of the domestic currency, and would not increase the burden of current debtors who repay their loans with a currency clause. The decision to introduce diversified money would significantly increase economic efficiency and quickly raise all economic parameters. An example of how this would impact Croatia and the U.S. is demonstrated in Tables 7 and 8.

Table 7: Increase in Croatian Exports in 2008 with the
Introduction of Diversified Money (in thousands of dollars)

Mark	Country	Exports before introduction of diversified money	Exports after introduction of diversified money	Increase of exports after introduction of diversified money
01	Austria	815,658	1,162,426	346,768
02	Belgium	88,836	199,746	110,910
03	France	148,097	389,705	241,608
04	Italy	297,548	649,060	351,512
05	Germany	2,694,137	3,976,413	1,282,276
06	Russia	1,518,133	2,817,012	1,298,879
07	Japan	186,208	1,693,538	1,507,330
08	China	60,800	250,183	189,383
09	Turkey	36,254	961,044	924,790
10	Morocco	88,315	282,674	194,359
11	USA	10,590	71,660	61,070
12	Taiwan	350,228	487,851	137,623
	Total	**6,294,804**	**12,941,312**	**6,646,508**

Table 8: Increase in U.S. Exports in 2005 with the Introduction of Diversified Money (in billions of dollars)

Mark	Country	Export before introduction of diversified money	Exports after introduction of diversified money	Increase of exports after introduction of diversified money
01	Canada	211.9	251.2	39.3
02	Mexico	120.4	145.3	24.9
03	Japan	55.5	96.8	41.3
04	China	41.9	142.7	100.8
05	UK	38.6	44.8	6.2
06	Germany	34.2	59.5	25.3
07	South	27.8	35.8	8.0
08	Korea	26.5	13.3	13.2
09	Netherlands	22.4	28.1	5.7
10	France	22.1	28.5	6.4
	Total	**601.3**	**846.0**	**244.70**

Croatia's foreign debt could be reduced from the foreign exchange earnings from tourism services, which is estimated at approximately 5.6 billion euros annually. The following table shows a hypothetical scenario for Croatia during the period from 2004-10.

Table 9: Trends in the External Debt of Croatia with the Introduction of Diversified Money (in millions of euros)

Year	Amount of the external debt	Index
2004	22.933	100
2005	17.333	75
2006	11.733	51
2007	6.133	27
2008	533	2
2009	0	0
2010	0	0

By applying the principle of diversified money, Croatia would also solve the issue of the profitability of the shipbuilding and wood processing industries, as well as all of its other exports. This principle should be applied to the so-called capillary imports. Diversified money would not be a contradiction to free international trade; only the importers who generate economic deviations would be excluded.

When assessing interstate trade, its usefulness for consumers and the country's economics should be distinguished. The usefulness of this trade is in expanding markets and increasing production volume, which results in lower costs and lower prices for the consumers, as estimated by some authors in their analysis of the international economy. However, this is only true if the trade between countries is balanced or when no deficit exists in either of the partner countries. In terms of the equilibrium of the balance of payments, the exchange rate of the diversified money would correspond to the exchange rate of regular money. Diversified money is a useful tool to prevent economic deviations.

5.2 Current Account of Diversified Money

Financial business abroad should be carried out through a special bank account with diversified money. This account should be open to any person who acquires business abroad. The process of opening and entering such an account is described below.

(1) Opening a Diversified Transfer Account

Diversified bank transfer accounts in Croatia should be opened by persons engaged in legal exports or imports. These separate accounts for each foreign country would be opened at commercial banks. The diversified bank transfer accounts have a depository relationship with the bank and the operations through them should be made in domestic currency.

(2) Payment of Exports

All payments for exports should be arranged through an appropriate letter of credit in favor of the diversified bank transfer account for that country. Granting credit to foreign buyers should not be allowed.

(3) The Conversion of the Payments from Exports

After the payment of the foreign buyer to the diversified bank transfer account of the exporter, the commercial bank converts the received amount into the diversified amount according to its exchange rate. By this, domestic currency is converted into domestic diversified currency, which is applied only to transactions with a particular foreign country. For example, kunas for Croatia are converted into kunas for Italy.

(4) *The Sale of Diversified Money*

After the import contract has been concluded or the preliminary calculation for the importation from a foreign country has been received, the importer gives the order to his commercial bank to sell him the domestic currency for this country in the required amount. If the commercial bank has the currency available for that country in its diversified bank transfer account, it then issues a statement of accounts for the sale of the diversified amount of the currency.

For example, for imports of 100 kunas from Country X, the importer must pay the diversified equivalent of 122 kunas. Upon payment of that amount, the importer will receive 100 kunas from his commercial bank in his diversified transfer account, with which he can execute the import from Country X. At the same time, the commercial bank will pay the exporter 120 kunas in its current business account, keeping two kunas as its commission. Such a procedure ensures that importers can only import the value that was created by the exporters.

To simplify the business, authorized persons may purchase diversified money from commercial banks for imports from Country X prior to the agreed import, and keep it in their diversified bank account for Country X and pay for the imported goods with special bank cards issued for that diversified transfer account.

(5) *Announcement of the Diversified Exchange Rate*

The diversified exchange rates are determined by the ratio of imports and exports for the previous month for each country. The relationship between the imports and exports of Croatia in 2008 are shown in Table 10.

Table 10: The Ratio of Imports and Exports

Mark	Country	Export	Import	The ratio of imports and exports {4:3} = 5
1	2	3	4	5
001	Austria	815.658	1,509.195	1.8503
002	Belgium	88.836	310.656	3.4970
003	Czech Republic	148.097	631.313	4.2628
004	France	297.548	1,000.572	3.3627
005	Italy	2,694.137	5,258.688	1.9519
006	Germany	1,518.133	4,115.890	2.7111
007	Russia	186.208	3,200.867	17.1897
008	Japan	60.800	439.566	7.2297
009	China	36.254	1,885.833	52.0172
010	Turkey	88.315	477.033	5.4015
011	USA	350.228	625.474	1.7859

(6) *The Form of Diversified Bank Accounts*

Diversified bank accounts have an expanded classical form of bookkeeping T-bills. They look like this:

Table 11: Diversified Bank Account of Exports

Business bank: A-B, Zagreb
Exporter: Alpha, Zagreb
The Country Exports: 006
Payment Currency: Euro

Document number and date	Value of exports in kunas	Payment of the purchased goods in kunas	Sold amount diversified value in kunas	The rest of the diversified values in kunas
		Debit	Credit	Balance
In 10/2010 30.11.10.	700.000,00	1,141.000,00	841.000,00	300.000,00
In 15/2010 14.12.10.	300.000,00	480.000,00	700.000,00	80.000,00
TOTAL	1,000.000,00	1,621.000,00	1,541.000,00	80.000,00

Table 12: Diversified Bank Account of Imports

Business bank: A-B, Zagreb
Exporter: Beta, Zagreb
The Country Exports: 006
Payment Currency: Euro

Document number and date	Purchased amount in kunas	Payment of the purchased goods in kunas	
	Debit	Credit	Balance
In 78/2010 05.12.10.	600,000.00	540,000.00	60,000.00
In 96/2010 20.12.10.	400,000.00	455,000.00	5,000.00
TOTAL	1,000,000.00	995,000.00	5,000.00

(7) Comments on the Negative Remainder of the Diversified Bank Transfer Account of Imports

A deficit in interstate commerce is an economic deviation. In some cases it can be justified if the deviation occurred due to the buying of technology for the creation of economic duals, the products and economic fruits of which will enable the users to repay the developed debt within the regular terms, regardless of the state. If the deviation is the result of the purchase of consumer goods that do not create economic micro-duals then it is unjustified and harmful, because the state will have to pay the deficit from its property or at the expense of the future consumption in the country.

(8) The Relationship of the Normal and the Diversified Exchange Rate

The general exchange rate of a currency is subject to daily economic fluctuations of the principle of supply and demand. These oscillations may be depreciated or appreciated. The diversified exchange rate is not a general currency exchange rate. It is an exchange rate that emerges from interstate trade, is determined separately for each country, and is determined monthly, not daily. This exchange rate can only be higher than the general exchange rate.

(9) The Freedom of Interstate Trade

The diversified exchange rate affects the volume of interstate trade of every country, with any other partner country separately, and only on the principle of the quantity of the imports and exports, as well as the supply and the demand of diversified money. In fact, there is no trade discrimination against any country. This instrument produces steady interstate commerce. It is important to note that the application of this principle does not disturb any of the principles of free trade between the states. It serves only to eliminate trade deviations.

(10) The Behavior of the Exporter

When introducing the principle of diversified money in interstate trade, every exporter behaves economically rationally. He directs his exports to that country for which the largest diversification coefficient was published (if other conditions do not prevent such orientation). The exporter will then achieve the best financial result, and the deficit of the exporting country will be decreased more rapidly with countries where there is currently the largest deficit. When the exports and imports of the partner countries become balanced, then the diversification exchange rate becomes equal to the general exchange rate. When this happens with all countries, the economic deviation generated from the imbalance of the export and import of the state will be completely eliminated and there will be no need to use diversified money.

(11) The Behavior of the Importer

The behavior of the importer will be the opposite of the exporter. The import will be directed to that country for which the minimum diversification coefficient was published (if all other conditions allow such a choice).

(12) The Economic Results

The diversification exchange rates will have more economic effects. They will be both positive and negative and will apply to the exporters, the importers, the state, and the citizens.

(13) The Effects on Exporters

The effects on the exporters are positive. The export prices and income are increased, as long as the coefficients of diversification for the country to which they export are greater than one. When the diversification coefficients become one, the positive effects end.

(14) The Effects on Importers

The effects on the importers are not positive. The import prices and expenditures increase as long as the coefficients of diversification for the countries from which they import are more than one. When the coefficients of diversification become one, the negative effects cease.

(15) The Effects for the Debtor Country

Several positive effects for the debtor state will be generated:

- Current account deficits in transactions with certain foreign countries are eliminated.
- Foreign countries are forced to cover the imports by exports, thus equalizing the diversification rate of exchange with the general exchange rate, and making their exports viable.
- An increase in the volume of production and employment in the debtor country is made possible.
- Contributes to the increase in gross domestic product and tax revenues in the debtor country.
- Exempts the debtor country from the interest costs on the amount of the payment deficit.
- In a time of economic deviations, export companies become more profitable.
- Profits and purchasing power in the debtor state are increased.
- Economic power of the debtor state strengthens.

(16) The Effects on the Citizens of the Debtor State

The effects on the citizens of the debtor state in times of economic deviations are partly unfavorable because the imported goods become more expensive for the consumer. On the other hand, they are positive because the possibility of domestic production and reduction of the unemployed is increased.

(17) Calculation and Determination of Diversified Exchange Rates

The basis for calculating and determining the diversified exchange rates is the diversification coefficient and the assessment of the importance of the economic relations with individual foreign countries. Considering that diversification exchange rates are issued and published every month, the rate can be easily adapted to the current state of economic relations. In the following table, the diversification coefficients of Croatia are given for states that were its main foreign trade partners at the end of 2008.

Table 13: Diversification Coefficients of Croatia

The State	The ratio of imports and exports	The importance of economic relations	Diversification coefficients	Market-adjusted coefficient
001	1.850	0.70	1.2952	1.3000
002	3.497	0.50	1.7485	1.7500
003	4.263	0.40	1.7051	1.7000
004	3.363	0.40	1.3451	1.4000
005	1.952	0.90	1.7567	1.8000
006	2.711	0.70	1.8978	1.8978
007	17.190	0.20	3.4379	3.6000
008	7.230	0.30	2.1689	2.1000
009	52.017	0.10	5.2017	6.0000
010	5.402	0.50	2.7008	2.7008
011	12.533	0.20	2.5067	2.5000
012	1.786	0.90	1.6073	1.6073

The diversification exchange rates of Croatia for individual states should be determined by the commercial banks in accordance with the Croatian National Bank.

(18) Limits of Resources

Due to the fact that importers from certain countries can only pay with the diversified money for these countries, their financial means are a limited economic resource subject to supply and demand. This resource can be bought by importers at a monthly diversified exchange rate or an exchange rate that is corrected by the market if so dictated by reasons of supply and demand.

(19) The Control of Imports

The legal importing of goods from abroad during customs clearance will also need to have a document attached on the payment of these goods from the diversified bank transfer account.

(20) Conclusions

Based on the analysis of the concept of diversified money, several conclusions can be made:

1. By diversification, the domestic currency for export is temporarily appreciated for each foreign country in a different intensity, depending on the imbalance of imports and exports, while for the importers it depreciates.
2. The purpose of the temporary export appreciation and import depreciation is the price increase of

imports from individual foreign countries and the support of exports to those countries.

3. The purpose of the temporary appreciation and depreciation is the balance of exports and imports.

4. The degree of appreciation and depreciation depends on the size of the imbalance of the trade imbalance, meaning that a greater imbalance causes a higher degree of exchange rate changes.

5. Appreciation and depreciation are set so that the fastest balance in the imports and exports is achieved with those countries where the imbalance is the greatest.

6. Once the balance of imports and exports is achieved, the temporary appreciation and depreciation for imports and exports is abolished and the general daily exchange rate is used.

7. By using diversified money the partner countries are economically compelled to eliminate economic deviations resulting from the imbalance of imports and exports.

6. Amortization of State Budget Debts

The state budget is the largest economic entity in each country and the holder of its main economic characteristics. It generates influence, as well as economic benefits and burdens. Its main economic benefits are reflected by the purchasing power of the country and a large part of the country's consumption. Its main economic burdens are incorporated in the prices of all material goods and services produced in the country.

The balance of the major benefits and burdens generated by the budget is different for each country. It depends on the size of the state and the structure of production in each country. States do not prepare for such a precise balance. Politicians running for office do not calculate the exact economic impact that their programs will generate. This often leads to unintended consequences. Politicians are famous for saying such things as "I hate taxes" and "We do not need an austerity policy." The result of such policies is states going into debt. The immediate consequences of that are huge profits for banks, huge speculative profits, markedly increased stratification in society, rising inflation, increased unreasonable spending of economic resources, and increasing political tensions and civil deviation. If the state budget is based on the economic rationality, then it is positive and its result will be a universal economic balance. If the state budget is not based on economic rationality, and its structure successively incorporates loans for consumption without foundation in purchasing power derived from the production of economic resources, then it is negative and will result in damage to the state.

The revenues and expenditures of the state are economically balanced if its revenues rise only from economic duals. When the balance of revenue and expenditures is not balanced, and when the income raised from economic duals is less than the expenditures and must be balanced by going into debt, then there is no economic balance, only financial. Problems with debts then begin and that is an economic deviation.

6.1 The Economic Balance of the State Budget

In creating the state budget we must start from the premise that the revenue structure is formed and then deal with the structure of expenditures. The income structure is formed by the various tax bases passed into law. Once you have established the revenue, the expenditures are formed. They should be somewhat lower than the revenue so that budgetary financial reserves may be established or increased out of the difference. A state budget formed this way is an economic calculation. In the realization of the state budget during the year unforeseeable circumstances may occur that could cause some of the line items in the budget to be exceeded in value. The budgetary financial reserves are used for the remediation of such overruns.

A state budget structured this way has an economic balance and is a positive budget. It does not violate the legal rights of economic agents in the market, does not jeopardize the safety functions financed by the budget, and does not cause disturbances in the functioning of the economic system of the country.

Politicians often form the state budget forming the expenditure side first and incorporating the expenses of their political programs. Only after that do they form the revenue side, restoring the missing amount by borrowing money. In principle, this is detrimental to the state's economy. In fact, many politicians have no competent ideas about how to form a budget.

6.2 Effects of Economic Duals in the Repayment of State Budget Debt

The credit debt of the state budget can be paid in two ways. The first is by the use of economic duals and the other is by reducing expenditures. The first way is better because it increases development. Attempting to reduce expenses causes political problems and the possibility of economic progress narrows. For this reason, only the method of applying economic duals and the positive effects arising from it will be further described.

Economic Micro-Duals

The ability to sell resources is created by their production and the demand by created purchasing power. The media for the synchronization of these two economic poles are the market and money. The system also includes economic and technological micro-duals. An economic dual is essentially an economic "atom" that makes up any economic organism. These atoms are constantly generated and extinguished. Their creation and extinction result in economic fruits. Based on the nature of entrepreneurship, the primary economic fruit is profit and the secondary is purchasing power (income or revenue).

While every business deal on the market is not an economic micro-dual, they create new products and services for the market. When a country intervenes by increasing supply or demand in a form that is different than the economic micro-dual it produces an economic deviation. It increases the number of economic satellites that are not transformed into an economic core, and only increase the volume of the satellites of consumption in future economic micro-duals. This measure brings short term benefits but causes long term damage. This can only be done on a temporary basis and on a very limited scale.

To make a complex of economic activities have the properties of a micro-economic dual, it must fulfill four conditions:

(1) It consists of an economic core and economic satellites.
(2) Both activities are carried out in the same economic space.
(3) The economic core has the ability to turn into an economic satellite.
(4) Some of the economic satellites have the ability to turn into an economic core.

Take the purchase of an apartment for example. When a customer buys an apartment for his personal housing it is consumption. When a customer buys an apartment to rent on the market it is an economic micro-dual, because they use the apartment as a means to produce services for the market, thereby creating economic fruits in the form of profit and purchasing power. The economic policy of the state should distinguish between these two facts. If the minister of economy of a country does not do so he could contribute to the generation of economic deviations. The structure of economic micro-duals is shown in Table 14.

Table 14: The Structure of Economic Micro-duals

The economic core		The economic satellites	
Production of material good 'A'	1000	Payments for basic materials	220
		Payments for auxiliary materials	80
		Payment for electricity	40
		Payment for energy	30
		Payment for various services	60
		Payment of amortization	40
		Payment of rent	80
		Payment of net salaries	150
		Contributions on salaries	130
		Payment of various taxes	90
		Payment of interest	80
	1000		1000

Economic micro-duals can provide different economic effects important in allowing the state to repay debts. Some of these conceptual effects will be more broadly shown below.

In Table 14 and Figure 1, it can be seen that the economic value of the core is equal to the cost price of the product A, and the value of the cost price of the product is equal to the sum of the sale values of individual economic satellites. Consequently, the value of an economic micro-dual is constituted of two halves of equal value. The dual equality of values constitutes the essence of all economic relations. If this equality is disturbed, there becomes an economic deviation. Figure 1 below shows a pictorial representation of the micro-duals. The right half is the economic core, and left shows the economic duals, displayed in different colors according to their share values.

Figure 1

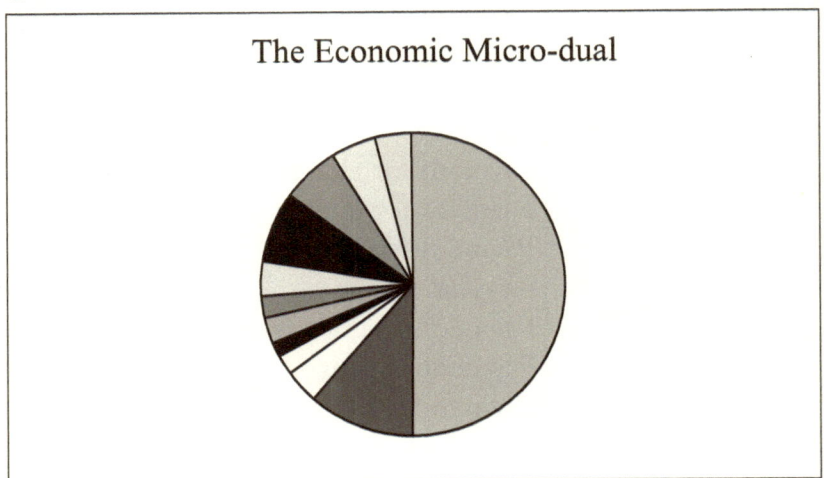

The Economic Micro-dual

Economic satellites that have the ability to turn into an economic core are reproductive and have two economic fruit—profit and purchasing power. Those that do not have this ability are satellites of consumption and have only one economic fruit, purchasing power. Economic satellites can be compared with beehives. Hives are made up of workers and drones. The latter are necessary only for the fertilization of the queen bee but are a burden to the hive. The importance of economic micro-duals for the state economy is estimated by the value of the share of the reproductive economic satellites in it. Part of the economic satellites is final consumption (taxes, contributions, and interest). They are a necessary economic burden of production, because they only increase investments into the economic core. They are not converted into new economic cores for the production of new products to be offered on the market directly after payment.

The economic core of the hive is the production of honey. One type of bees takes care of the queen bee and do not produce honey. Another kind of bees is taking care of the offspring. They also do not produce honey. The third type is the guardians of the hive. They also do not produce honey. The fourth kind are drones who just fertilize the queen. They do not produce honey. All these categories are necessary burdens of the apiary.

Only one part of the bee population produces honey and they constantly reproduce their function till their death. The example of drones is used as an illustration for final consumption which is a necessary burden of the hive. The shares of reproductive satellites in the total number of satellites in particular types of economic activities are shown in Table 15.

Ivan Ovcaricek-Rostok

Table 15: Value of the Share of Economic Satellites in Economic Micro-Duals

Shares of economic satellites	Production of material goods	Trade services with domestic products	Tourism services with domestic components	Transport services
The share of reproductive economic satellites	0.4 – 0.6	0.3 – 0.4	0.2 – 0.4	0.1 – 0.2
The share of economic satellites of consumption	0.4 – 0.6	0.6- 0.7	0.6 – 0.8	0.8 – 0.9

According to indicators of the value share of reproductive economic satellites in economic micro-duals, the most important factor in a country's economy is the production of material products, followed by the production of services in the trade of domestic products, the production of tourism services with domestic components, and ultimately the production of traffic services (freight and transport). The quantity of the economic fruits depends on the frequency of the creation and extinction of the economic micro-duals over the course of a year. Increasing the frequency of their creation and extinction also increases the amount of their economic fruit. This frequency depends on whether the created product is immediately sold or put into the inventory for later sale.

The cost price of the economic core is equal to the sum of the sale and accounting values of the economic satellites. It achieves its profit when it becomes a reproductive (economic) satellite of consumption. By its monetary payments, the economic core creates purchasing power for the demand of goods on the market. With the payment, the economic fruits contained in the satellites are realized. If there was no profit in the economic satellites, the volume of economic activity would be steady. If a loss was included in the economic satellites, the volume of economic activity would be in a regressive state. In some economic satellites, profits and loss can be created. Micro-duals containing a loss are detrimental to the economic system.

The duration of economic micro-duals is determined by the duration of the core and the satellites. In modern economy, the duration of the economic core has been established as one month, and the duration of the economic satellites as one extended week (ten days). The duration of the satellites should be taken as a standard based on general usage. The duration of the economic core corresponds to the accounting period in the production, and the duration of the economic satellites corresponds to the payment deadline. Considering the total duration of a standard economic micro-dual of forty days (the duration of the core plus satellite), it mean that nine such economic micro-duals can be realized in a year.

The frequency of the creation of the micro-duals is very important for the state economy. Micro-duals that last longer than the standard of forty days bear a smaller amount of total economic fruit, so it is in the interest of every country to monitor their frequency of formation and structure its regulations to stick to the forty day standard or increase it. The increase could be facilitated by rationalization and modernization of production technologies and by prescription of shorter payment terms. If the duration of the economic micro-duals is more than forty days, it is a sign that the production sector in the country has problems. Those problems could begin to move into the economic system of the state, thus causing the slowing of economic functions and the reduction of the economic fruits. In this case, the state should intervene with "therapy," regulations to stop the spread of the "infection." The positive and negative aspects of economic micro-duals are shown in Table 16.

Table 16: Usefulness of Economic Micro-Duals

Type of the economic Micro-Duals	Useful	Partially useful	Adverse
Micro-duals with profit and a duration up to 40 days	X		
Micro-duals with profit and a duration of 41-90 days		X	
Micro-duals without profit and a duration up to 40 days		X	
Micro-duals with profit and a duration of 91 or more days			X
Micro-duals with loss			X

Economic micro-duals are useful for the state when there is a gain and they last up to forty days. They are partially useful when lasting forty-one to ninety days, and are harmful when lasting more than ninety days or result in a monetary loss. Harmful micro-duals can be restored and converted into useful ones, or thrown out of the state's economic system to improve its health.

Types of economic micro-duals

There are two basic types of economic micro-duals in the economic life of a country, reproductive and consumption, and one that is a combination of both. When the economic core is formed by material products or services, and when all payments for used components in the production are done, a micro-dual is formed. When this form comes to the market it changes its essence and becomes an economic satellite in some other production or in consumption. The amount of material products or services that enter other productions become reproductive satellites. If they become consumables they become economic satellites of consumption.

For example, paper can be a component in the manufacturing process of printing books, an item of expenditure for writing documents in offices, or for writing in households. Material products that fail to be sold, or services that are not useful to anyone, become economic waste. If the payments for the used components in the production of material products or services are not made, an economic deviation forms. Economic duals then remain unfinished and the process of their reproduction and multiplication is interrupted. Such conditions are the result of disregarding a concluded contract or are economic fraud. These should be subject to legal sanctions, either as organized restriction of trade or criminal acts of fraud. Non-payments destroy the stability of any economic system.

6.3 Effects of Multiplication of the Economic Micro-Duals

Economic micro-duals continually rise and disappear. The frequency of the emergence and disappearance is different depending on the length of time they exist. Their cycles over the course of a year are called the multiplication of economic micro-duals. The result of multiplication is the annual number of realized micro-duals. If each of these micro-duals gives economic fruit, then the amount of fruit is directly dependent on the number of realized micro-duals.

The Case of the Duration of Economic Micro-Duals of Forty Days

If an economic micro-dual lasts forty days then nine of its cycles can be realized in one year. If each of these micro-duals has an economic core with ten economic satellites, and if three of them in the next cycle turn into economic cores, then in the course of one year 9,840 new micro-duals are generated, a healthy increase in economic activity for any system. From this data we see the importance of the duration of an economic micro-dual. The calculation is shown in Table 17.

Table 17: Multiplication of the Micro-Duals in One Year

Duration: 40 days
Core/satellite: 1/10
Satellite/core: 10/3

Number of reproductions of the micro-duals	Number of economic cores	Number of economic satellites	Number of new economic micro-duals	Total number of new micro-duals (4+5)*
1	2	3	4	5
1	1	10	0	0
2	3	30	3	3
3	9	90	9	12
4	27	270	27	39
5	81	810	81	120
6	243	2,430	243	363
7	729	7,290	729	1,092
8	2,187	21,870	2,187	3,279
9	6,561	65,610	6,561	9,840

* The sum of the chain

The Case of the Duration of Economic Micro-Duals in Sixty Days

If the duration of an economic micro-dual is extended from forty days to sixty, the number of its cycles in one year will be reduced from nine to six, and the number of possible newly generated economic micro-duals will be reduced from 9,840 to

363, or twenty-seven times less. This is a geometric reduction that will reduce the economic fruits in the same proportion. The calculation is shown in Table 18.

Table 18: Multiplication of the Micro-Duals in One Year

Duration: 60 days
Core/satellite: 1/10
Satellite/core: 10/3

Number of reproductions of the micro-duals	Number of economic cores	Number of economic satellites	Number of new economic micro-duals	Total number of new micro-duals (4+5)*
1	2	3	4	5
1	1	10	0	0
2	3	30	3	3
3	9	90	9	12
4	27	270	27	39
5	81	810	81	120
6	243	2.430	243	363

* The sum of the chain

The Case of the Duration of Economic Micro-Duals in Ninety Days

If the duration of an economic micro-dual extends from forty days to ninety days then the number of its cycles in one year will be reduced from nine to four and the number of possible new generated economic micro-duals will be reduced from 9,840 to thirty-nine, or by 252 times. This will bring a corresponding reduction in the economic fruits. The calculation is shown in Table 19.

Table 19: Multiplication of the Micro-Duals in One Year

Duration: 90 days
Core/satellite: 1/10
Satellite/core: 10/3

Number of reproductions of the micro-duals	Number of economic cores	Number of economic satellites	Number of new economic micro-duals	Total number of new micro-duals (4+5)*
1	2	3	4	5
1	1	10	0	0
2	3	30	3	3
3	9	90	9	12
4	27	270	27	39

* The sum of the chain

If these calculations are translated to a country's economics, we see their aggregate impact on its economic success. For that reason, each country should prescribe a standard duration of economic micro-duals that is related to the duration of economic satellites—that is, the term of all payments.

Figure 2

The Case of Multiplication of Economic Micro-Duals in Croatia

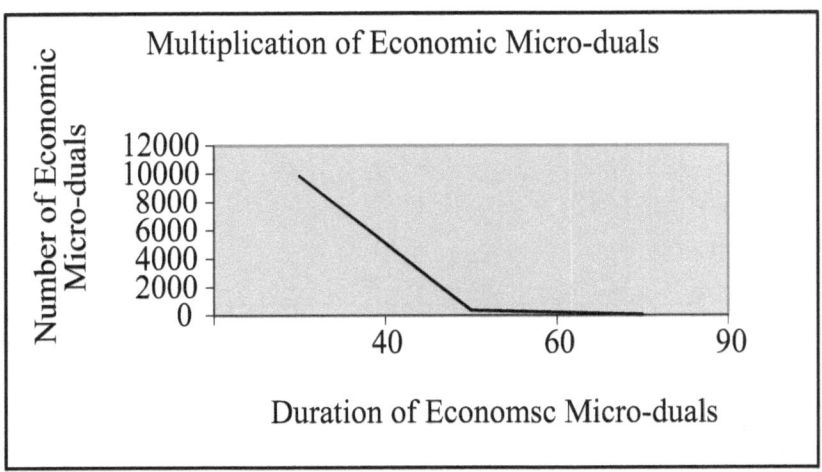

As an example, we can take a look at the data for Croatia. In 2008, the multiplication of economic micro-duals had an average cycle of about sixty-two days, with twelve economic satellites. At first glance, these cycles were satisfactory, but large economic reserves were hidden in them. They were held at that level because of foreign loans. This is shown in Table 20.

Table 20: Multiplication of the Micro-Duals in Croatia, 2008

Duration: 62 days
Core/satellite: 1/12
Satellite/core: 12/3

Number of reproductions of the micro-duals	Number of economic cores	Number of economic satellites	Number of new economic micro-duals	Total number of new micro-duals (4+5) *
1	2	3	4	5
1	1	12	0	0
2	3	36	3	3
3	9	108	9	12
4	27	324	27	39
5	81	972	81	120
6	243	2916	243	363

* The sum of the chain

If foreign loans were excluded, then the duration of these cycles would be extended to about seventy-three days. In that case, the effects of the multiplication would be weaker. This is illustrated in Table 21.

Table 21: Multiplication of the Micro-Duals in Croatia, 2008

Duration: 73 days
Core/satellite: 1/12
Satellite/core: 12/3

Number of reproductions of the micro-duals	Number of economic cores	Number of economic satellites	Number of new economic micro-duals	Total number of new micro-duals (4+5)*
1	2	3	4	5
1	1	10	0	0
2	3	30	3	3
3	9	90	9	12
4	27	270	27	39
5	81	810	81	120

* The sum of the chain

If the standard multiplication is taken as an optimum for Croatia (a micro-dual with a duration of forty days), the ratio of core to satellites is 1:12, and the ratio of satellites to core is 12:3. The comparison would then show a large discrepancy. The total number of new micro-duals in one year at the optimum is 9,840, but in Croatia it would be 120, eighty-two times less than optimum. There is an enormous reserve of economic success. The above mathematical calculations were based on an economic micro-dual where one economic core has ten or twelve satellites and that three of them are turned into economic cores in a new cycle.

The Case of Multiplication of Economic Micro-Duals at Increasing the Number of Reproductive Economic Satellites

If the calculation of multiplication was made for an economic micro-dual greater than the standard, in which one economic core has twenty satellites, and four of them turn into economic cores in the new cycle, then the number of new economic micro-duals would increase 4.4 times. That is geometric growth. This multiplication is shown in Table 22.

Table 22: Multiplication of the Micro-Duals in One Year

Duration: 40 days
Core/satellite: 1/20
Satellite/core: 20/4

Number of reproductions of the micro-duals	Number of economic cores	Number of economic satellites	Number of new economic micro-duals	Total number of new micro-duals (4+5)*
1	2	3	4	5
1	1	20	0	0
2	4	80	4	4
3	16	160	16	20
4	32	640	32	52
5	128	2,560	128	180
6	512	10,240	512	692
7	2,048	40,960	2,048	2,740

Number of reproductions of the micro-duals	Number of economic cores	Number of economic satellites	Number of new economic micro-duals	Total number of new micro-duals (4+5)*
8	8,192	163,840	8,192	10,932
9	32,768	655,360	32,768	43,700

* The sum of the chain

If the calculation was made for the same size of the economic micro-dual, but five economic satellites were turned into cores in the next cycle, then the number of new economic micro-duals would grow eleven times, as seen in Table 23.

Table 23: Multiplication of the Micro-Duals in One Year

Duration: 40 days
Core/satellite: 1/20
Satellite/core: 20/5

Number of reproductions of the micro-duals	Number of economic cores	Number of economic satellites	Number of new economic micro-duals	Total number of new micro-duals (4+5)*
1	2	3	4	5
1	1	20	0	0
2	5	100	5	5

Number of reproductions of the micro-duals	Number of economic cores	Number of economic satellites	Number of new economic micro-duals	Total number of new micro-duals (4+5)*
3	25	500	25	30
4	125	2,500	125	155
5	625	12,500	625	780
6	3,125	62,500	3,124	3,905
7	15,625	312,500	15,625	19,530
8	78,125	1,562.500	78,125	97,655
9	390,625	7,812.500	390,625	488,280

* The sum of the chain

Figure 3

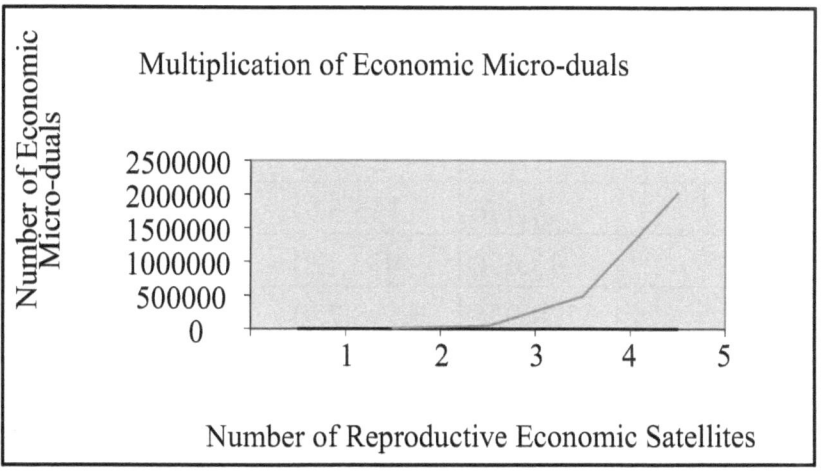

If we assume that six economic satellites for this size of economic micro-dual turn into economic cores in a new cycle, then the number of new micro-duals would grow forty-six times, as seen in Table 24.

Table 24: Multiplication of the Micro-Duals in One Year

Duration: 40 days
Core/satellite: 1/20
Satellite/core: 20/6

Number of reproductions of the micro-duals	Number of economic cores	Number of economic satellites	Number of new economic micro-duals	Total number of new micro-duals (4+5)*
1	2	3	4	5
1	1	20	0	0
2	6	120	6	6
3	36	720	36	42
4	216	1,296	216	258
5	1,296	25,920	1,296	1,554
6	7,776	155,520	7,776	9,330
7	46,656	933,120	46,656	55,986
8	279,936	5,598,720	279,936	335,922
9	1,679,616	33,592,320	1,679,616	2,015,538

* The sum of the chain

These data show that it is very important for the state to stimulate production of things that have a larger number of economic satellites because they geometrically multiply business and potential economic fruits. In Croatia, this specifically refers to shipbuilding, the electrical industry, production of rolling stock, and large-scale construction.

When considering the question of economic micro-duals, their various sizes and the lengths of duration are important, but it must be recognized that the size of the micro-dual depends on the average development of the technology of the production and its economic orientation. However, the duration of economic satellites also depends on whether the state will prescribe rational payment terms and legally shorten their duration. The importance is demonstrated by a hypothetical assumption that the payment period is zero days (that prompt payment is realized), whereby the duration of the standard economic micro-dual of forty days is reduced to thirty. In that case, twelve of its cycles are realized in one year, resulting in an increase in the total number of new micro-duals from 9,840 to 265,719, twenty-seven times greater. This multiplication is seen in Table 25.

Table 25: Multiplication of the Micro-Duals in One Year

Duration: 30 days
Core/satellite: 1/10
Satellite/core: 10/3

Number of reproductions of the micro-duals	Number of economic cores	Number of economic satellites	Number of new economic micro-duals	Total number of new micro-duals (4+5) *
1	2	3	4	5
1	1	10	0	0
2	3	30	3	3
3	9	90	9	12
4	27	270	27	39
5	81	810	81	120
6	243	2.430	243	363
7	729	7.290	729	1.092
8	2.187	21.870	2.187	3.279
9	6.561	65.610	6.561	9.840
10	19.683	196.830	19.683	29.523
11	59.049	590.490	59.049	88.572
12	177.147	1,771.470	177.147	265.719

* The sum of the chain

Figure 4

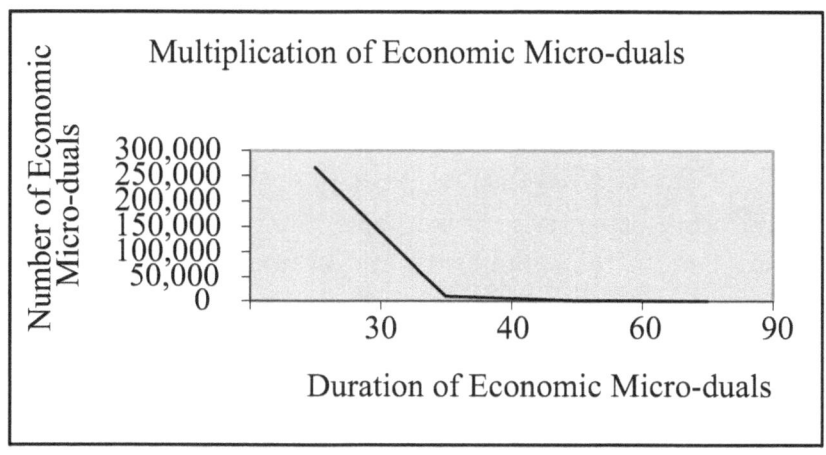

6.4 Effects in Economic Macro-Duals

The economic macro-dual is an aggregate (complex unity) of economic micro-duals created during a time period and in a limited economic space. The macro-dual has all the elements contained in its micro-duals. It also has an economic balance determined by a separate calculation. In the calculation, the aggregate elements that make up the balance between the economic resources of production and payment are determined. This calculation is important in determining the economic situation of the country. The economic macro-dual has the structure of a normal bookkeeping account, with the aggregated structure of the economic production resources on the left side, the structure of payments on the right. It is easy to understand the calculation.

When speaking about the economic resources of production, the aggregate value of all goods and services produced in a period of time, usually a month, quarter, or year, and in an economic space, the state or territorial unit, is understood. In economic theory these resources are also called *complex products*. The term *payment* implies the aggregate amount of money that is received as payment for delivered and settled elements used in the aggregated production. The aggregated structure of production (the complex economic core) includes the basic and auxiliary materials, electrical, energy, services, depreciation, rentals, net wages, contributions, expenses for taxes, and interest charges. All these costs are paid to the suppliers of the economic elements created by production. Aggregate costs for basic and auxiliary materials, electricity, and energy are paid to the suppliers of those elements. Aggregate depreciation costs are paid to a special account for the replacement of spent fixed assets. Aggregate costs for salaries are paid to employees. Aggregate contributions are paid to funds and various other subjects, and the aggregate costs of taxes to the budget. From this it can be seen that the purchasing power and demand arise from the production of economic resources. This is basic economic principle and regularity.

Scheme 1: Economic Macro-Duals

Aggregate of values of supply	Aggregate of values of demand
Production costs - basic materials - various ancillary materials - electricity - energy - various services - depreciation - rent	Payments received for delivery - basic materials - ancillary materials - electricity - for energy - for various services - depreciation

Aggregate of values of supply	Aggregate of values of demand
- salaries - contributions - taxes - interest	- for rent - salaries - to contribute - taxes - interest
Total supply	Total demand

Scheme 2: Economic Macro-duals: The Case of a Positive Balance

Aggregate of values of supply	Aggregate of values of demand
Production costs - basic materials - various ancillary materials - electricity - energy - various services - depreciation - rent - salaries - contributions - taxes - interest	Payments received for delivery - basic materials - ancillary materials - electricity - for energy - for various services - depreciation - for rent - salaries - to contribute - taxes - interest
Costs of imports Value of export	Payments for imports Payments for exports
Total supply value	Total demand value

The existence of outstanding payments and the cost of imports by exports in the economic macro-dual is a deviation in the economics of the state. It is a complex deviation, which produces two economic impacts: illiquidity and inflation. This is shown in Scheme 3.

Scheme 3: Economic Macro-Duals: The Case of a Negative Balance

Aggregate of value of supply	Aggregate of values of demand
Production costs - basic materials - various ancillary materials - electricity - energy - various services - depreciation - rent - salaries - contributions - taxes - interest	Payments received for delivery - basic materials - ancillary materials - electricity - for energy - for various services - depreciation - for rent - salaries - to contribute - taxes - interest
Cost of imports Value of export	Payments for imports Payments for exports
Uncovered costs of imports exports (loss)	External debt (reduction of state property)
Total supply	**Total demand**

A good choice of economic duals increases the volume of payments to the state budget while increasing the number of employees expands market demand and consumption. Tax revenues are also increased because of this. Retention of tax expenses at the same level, while simultaneously increasing the revenue from the increased gross domestic product, creates the possibility of repayment of state budget debt.

Chapter 3

Deviations in Debt

7. Economic Un-sustainability of Debt

The basic principle before entering into any debt is that the benefit of the debt is greater than the burden by which the debt was accepted. This also applies to state debt. The debt supports the realization of an idea, and that idea should contain safe benefits. When it comes to state debt, this means positive financial effects. A one-time deposit into a business venture should bring benefits greater than the debt when that debt is repaid. In such a case, the state debt is sustainable. If the calculation shows that the benefit is less than the debt, then it is irrational to go into debt. A sustainable debt always shows that a better economic result can be achieved in an enterprise than would be achieved without debt. This also could be true for losses. If the loss is less with the acceptance of a credit debt, then such debt is justified, but it is not sustainable. Government policy should always assure that debt is sustainable. For political reasons, states often go into debt for consumption. Such a debt has no return function and is always unsustainable.

8. Constantly Growing Debts

States often incur debts that they are not able to return, and such debts are converted into so-called perpetual debt. They generally have a tendency to continuously grow. No state has exactly determined and proven the damaging effects of long-term debt for consumption. Sometimes debts are useful for national policy, but they should be short term, of a period of less than one year. Each national debt that is based on a longer repayment period than one year has a damaging credit inversion effect. The credit inversion depends on the size of the financial benefits of the loan and the frequency of successive lending.

9. The Credit Inversion

States often use credit to finance projects that are entrepreneurial in nature. This is the case with things like transport infrastructure (railways, roads, airports, large bridges, large tunnels), facilities for controlling water flow to prevent flooding, construction of hydroelectric power plants, construction of seaports, and other specific objects. The state always does this as long term indebtedness. Some direct or indirect financial benefit is realized with the newly built facilities, or it increases the growth of the gross domestic product, and that financial value is greater than the installments for the credit repayments. If this is so, then it is positive and rational. However, it often happens that the installments of repayment of the loan are greater than the financial benefit of the built assets. That then makes it a credit inversion because the debt causes economic damage to the state.

European Criterions

The European Union has introduced criteria for limiting the debt of individual states. The upper limit of debt is sixty percent of the gross domestic product, and the allowable annual deficit of the state budget is up to three percent. These criteria are, at their maximum sizes, mutually incompatible. If a country has a debt of sixty percent of the budget, then its budget cannot have any deficit because it will automatically exceed the upper limit of indebtedness.

10. The Risk of Passing the Debt into Eternal Debt

In order to give a good judgment on the indebtedness of a state budget, we should start from exact economic parameters. Here, these parameters will be shown as hypothetical cases.

The first of these cases is from the policies of the European Union. From the established parameters, the viability of the state budget can be determined by deduction. Elements of the formula for the calculation are:

- Increase of gross domestic product (G)
- The size of the debt of the state budget in relation to the size of the GDP (D)
- The size of the state budget in relation to the GDP (B)
- The amortization coefficient (T)
- Annual budget deficit (Y)

Specific sizes:

- D = 60%
- B = 38%

- Amortization coefficient (T) for a term of 20 years and an annual yield of 1% = 0.05541531
- Annual budget deficit (Y) = 0

The formula for calculating is:

$$G = \frac{D}{B} \times 100 \times T + Y$$

Plugging in the known numbers we get:

$$G = \frac{60}{38} \times 100 \times 0.05541531 + 0$$

$$G = 157.89 \times 0.05541531 + 0$$

$$G = 8.75\%.$$

This calculation shows that the debt could be amortized within the twenty year period *if* the annual budget deficits of each of those years is completely eliminated, and *if* the entire budget revenue from the increase of the gross domestic product of 8.75 percent is used to cover the state budget debt. This is practically impossible to achieve, and the debt could change into a state of eternal debt. After that it becomes a political question and government policies must decide how to approach the repayment of such debt.

By the same calculation, the sizes of the increase in gross domestic product in various forms can be calculated and the possibilities for debt repayment can be given.

Table 26: Government Bonds (10-3)

Maturity: 10 years
Annual yield : 3%
The amortization coefficient : 0.11723051
The state budget deficit : 0

Size of government debt in relation to the size of the gross domestic product (D) %	Size of the state budget in relation to the size of the gross domestic product (B) %	Factor of the transformation of the debt into the budget category $\frac{D}{B}$ (...... x 100)	Required annual growth in gross domestic product for the repayment of debt (G) % (3 x 0.117232051)
1	2	3	4
10	38	26.3	3.1
20	38	52.6	6.2
30	38	78.9	9.2
40	38	105.3	12.3
50	38	131.6	15.4
60	38	157.9	18.5

From the data in Table 26, it can be seen that government bonds could be issued under these conditions only to cover a loan that does not exceed a level of up to ten percent of the yearly gross domestic product.

Table 27: Government Bonds (20-3)

Maturity: 20 years
Annual yield: 3%
The amortization coefficient: 0.06721571
The state budget deficit: 0

Size of government debt in relation to the size of the gross domestic product (D) %	Size of the state budget in relation to the size of the gross domestic product (B) %	Factor of transformation debt into the budget category D (...... x 100) B	Required annual growth in gross domestic product for the repayment of debt (G) % (3 x 0.06721571)
1	2	3	4
10	38	26.3	1.8
20	38	52.6	3.5
30	38	78.9	5.3
40	38	105.3	7.1
50	38	131.6	8.8
60	38	157.9	10.6

The data in Table 27 show that government bonds could be issued under these conditions to cover the loan, which could not exceed a level of up to twenty percent of the yearly gross domestic product.

Table 28: Government Bonds (30-3)

Maturity: 30 years
Annual yield: 3%
The amortization coefficient: 0.05101926
The state budget deficit: 0

Size of government debt in relation to the size of the gross domestic product (D) %	Size of the state budget in relation to the size of the gross domestic product (B) %	Factor of transformation debt into the budget category $\frac{D}{B}$ (...... x 100)	Required annual growth in gross domestic product for the repayment of debt (G) % (3 x 0.05101926)
1	2	3	4
10	38	26.3	1.3
20	38	52.6	2.7
30	38	78.9	4.0
40	38	105.3	5.4
50	38	131.6	6.7
60	38	157.9	8.1

The data in Table 28 show that government bonds could be issued under these conditions to cover the loan, which could not exceed a level of up to twenty percent of the yearly gross domestic product.

Table 29: Government Bonds (10-4)

Maturity: 10 years
Annual yield: 4%
The amortization coefficient: 0.12329094
The state budget deficit: 0

Size of government debt in relation to the size of the gross domestic product (D) %	Size of the state budget in relation to the size of the gross domestic product (B) %	Factor of transformation debt into the budget category $\frac{D}{B}$ (...... x 100)	Required annual growth in gross domestic product for the repayment of debt (G) % (3 x 0.12329094)
1	2	3	4
10	38	26.3	3.2
20	38	52.6	6.5
30	38	78.9	9.7
40	38	105.3	13.0
50	38	131.6	16.2
60	38	157.9	19.5

The data in Table 29 show that government bonds could be issued under these conditions to cover the loan, which could not exceed a level of up to ten percent of the yearly gross domestic product.

Table 30: Government Bonds (20-4)

Maturity: 20 years
Annual yield: 4%
The amortization coefficient: 0.07358175
The state budget deficit: 0

Size of government debt in relation to the size of the gross domestic product (D) %	Size of the state budget in relation to the size of the gross domestic product (B) %	Factor of transformation debt into the budget category $\frac{D}{B}$ (...... x 100)	Required annual growth in gross domestic product for the repayment of debt (G) % {3 x 0.07358175}
1	2	3	4
10	38	26.3	1.9
20	38	52.6	3.9
30	38	78.9	5.8
40	38	105.3	7.7
50	38	131.6	9.7
60	38	157.9	11.6

The data in Table 30 show that government bonds could be issued under these conditions to cover the loan, which could not exceed a level of up to ten percent of the yearly gross domestic product.

Table 31: Government Bonds (30-4)

Maturity: 30 years
Annual yield: 4%
The amortization coefficient: 0.05783010
The state budget deficit: 0

Size of government debt in relation to the size of the gross domestic product (D) %	Size of the state budget in relation to the size of the gross domestic product (B) %	Factor of transformation debt into the budget category $\frac{D}{B}$ (...... x 100)	Required annual growth in gross domestic product for the repayment of debt (G) % (3 x 0,05783010)
1	2	3	4
10	38	26.3	1.5
20	38	52.6	3.0
30	38	78.9	4.6
40	38	105.3	6.1
50	38	131.6	7.6
60	38	157.9	9.1

The data in Table 31 show that government bonds could be issued under these conditions to cover the loan, which could not exceed a level of up to twenty percent of the yearly gross domestic product.

Table 32: Government Bonds (10-6)

Maturity: 10 years
Annual yield: 6%
The amortization coefficient: 0.13586796
The state budget deficit: 0

Size of government debt in relation to the size of the gross domestic product (D) %	Size of the state budget in relation to the size of the gross domestic product (B) %	Factor of transformation debt into the budget category $\frac{D}{B}$ (...... x 100)	Required annual growth in gross domestic product for the repayment of debt (G) % (3 x 0.13586796)
1	2	3	4
10	38	26.3	3.6
20	38	52.6	7.1
30	38	78.9	10.7
40	38	105.3	14.3
50	38	131.6	17.9
60	38	157.9	21.4

The data in Table 32 show that the government bonds could not be issued under these conditions to cover the loan.

The data in Tables 26-32 show that the government bonds would not be issued to cover the debt in the amount of sixty percent of yearly gross domestic product. The finance ministers of the debtor states do not have these calculations in mind when assuming state debt. Therefore, the fate of these debts is to become eternal unless the state sells its property for their repayment.

Table 33: Government Bonds (a possible real case scenario, 30-1)

Maturity: 30 years
Annual yield: 1%
The amortization coefficient: 0.03874811
The state budget deficit: 0

Size of government debt in relation to the size of the gross domestic product (D) %	Size of the state budget in relation to the size of the gross domestic product (B) %	Factor of transformation debt into the budget category $\frac{D}{B}$ (...... x 100)	Required annual growth in gross domestic product for the repayment of debt (G) % (3 x 0.03874811)
1	2	3	4
10	38	26.3	1.0
20	38	52.6	2.0
30	38	78.9	3.1
40	38	105.3	4.1
50	38	131.6	5.1
60	38	157.9	6.1

Figure 5

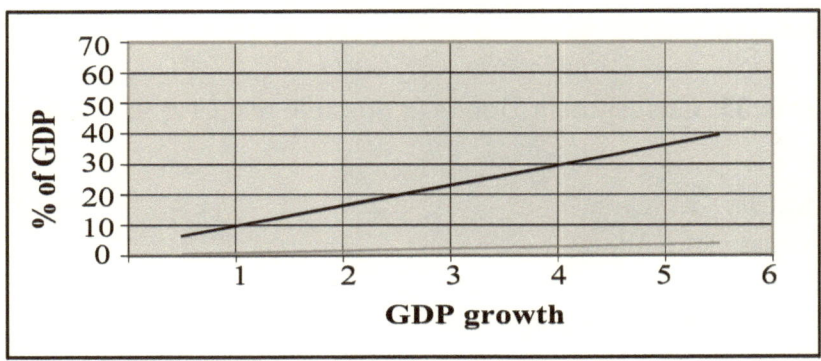

Government Bonds

The data in Table 33 show that government bonds could be issued under these conditions to cover the loan, which could not exceed a level of up to thirty percent of the yearly gross domestic product, in the amount of sixty percent of the gross domestic product, if half of the obligations could be paid from introducing diversified money in foreign trade.

11. External Debts of Countries

The foreign debt movements in some countries from 2003-10 are given in the following table. They all show rapid growth. From this we can conclude that stopping the global debt spiral will be a big problem because these debtors hold most of the world's economy.

Table 34: External Debt of Countries from 2003-2010 (in millions of dollars)

	Country	2003	2004	2005	2006	2007	2008	2009	2010
1	USA	6,946.289	8,353.479	9,476.403	11,204.108	13,427.103	13,749.570	13,767.867	14,456.194
2	UK	5,406.413	6,729.484	7,385.985	9,239.287	11,260.597	9,106.737	9,337.345	9,554.857
3	Germany	3,326.742	3,775.700	3,578.198	4,219.206	5,117.734	5,124.187	5,124.906	5,217.014
4	France	2,300.666	2,851.560	3,052.297	3,817.630	4,841.930	4,862.662	5,167.460	5,091.260
5	Japan	1,354.398	1,557.069	1,521.073	1,512.871	1,767.807	2,344.683	2,086.400	2,588.607
6	Italy	1,452.122	1,647.918	1,675.759	2,108.044	2,549.297	2,395.317	2,551.151	2,435.220
7	Netherlands	1,405.449	1,671.049	1,669.067	2,097.648	2,599.752	2,421.889	2,413.790	2,433.884
8	Spain	979.794	1,235.322	1,350.105	1,804.654	2,301.967	2,326.273	2,539.421	2,316.691
9	Ireland	734.333	1,052.149	1,336.187	1,763.130	2,267.387	2,355.639	2,384.730	2,303.419
10	Luxembourg	914.680	1,070.429	1,254.127	1,633.490	2,026.680	2,170.932	2,201.694	1,915.942
11	Belgium	777.777	961.460	984.755	1,155.691	1,535.057	1,595.147	1,436.925	1,292.068
12	Switzerland	807.631	906.949	886.947	1,041.639	1,452.517	1,230.334	1,252.839	1,287.359
13	Australia	419.006	506.062	532.343	639.634	820.413	799.838	1,035.746	1,167.884
14	Canada	579.614	605.532	633.907	696.612	831.729	839.608	997.474	1,106.998
15	Sweden	400.681	497.716	581.539	624.187	795.879	948.684	902.954	945.086
16	Hong Kong	372.708	430.121	454.594	516.382	711.057	663.373	668.484	803.416
17	Austria	408.806	492.980	510.795	646.036	801.400	832.753	831.601	797.790

	Country	2003	2004	2005	2006	2007	2008	2009	2010
18	Denmark	297.079	351.858	358.288	450.127	568.648	585.522	605.573	596.199
19	Norway	237.248	282.528	275.782	408.880	540.258	568.670	546.453	583.684
20	China	208.431	247.679	283.986	325.260	373.773	378.245	428.442	548.938
21	Greece	204.577	253.287	262.954	329.782	454.200	504.612	587.562	546.607
22	Portugal	270.454	310.627	302.220	381.453	483.916	484.710	549.149	528.597
23	Russia	185.741	214.503	257.402	313.176	463.915	480.541	467.245	489.043
24	Finland	185.709	227.518	218.723	264.020	316.256	346.073	406.367	441.369
25	South Korea	141.650	150.625	161.413	225.200	333.428	317.370	345.391	359.985
26	Brazil	235.005	219.786	187.526	193.458	237.605	262.931	277.563	351.941
27	India	117.872	122.587	120.224	158.493	202.793	229.271	252.398	295.891
28	Turkey	143.940	160.977	169.908	207.842	249.573	277.125	268.457	289.387
29	Poland	107.274	129.989	132.926	169.636	234.052	245.496	280.187	264.574
30	Mexico	170.847	171.162	167.942	162.497	192.689	200.393	200.213	250.956
31	Hungary	58.067	81.552	84.925	132.246	176.903	222.999	238.067	209.540
32	Indonesia	133.434	137.124	134.353	125.348	133.917	155.067	172.871	200.050
33	Argentina	160.278	162.379	124.939	115.863	117.317	128.112	116.415	128.600
34	Romania	22.627	29.574	38.861	54.432	85.422	100.247	118.582	122.994
35	United Arab Emir.	20.710	25.900	34.470	39.100	61.680	126.900	122.500	122.700

	Country	2003	2004	2005	2006	2007	2008	2009	2010
36	Iceland	16.095	26.553	46.141	74.910	119.216	68.612	121.135	119.435
37	Kazakhstan	22.884	32.713	43.429	74.014	96.914	108.130	113.239	119.242
38	Ukraine	23.811	30.647	39.619	54.512	79.955	101.659	103.396	117.346
39	Israel	74.059	78.423	78.151	87.418	90.116	86.948	92.109	106.018
40	Cyprus	7.439	12.613	14.686	24.395	28.257	26.456	119.522	103.585
41	Thailand	51.783	51.312	52.040	59.643	61.738	65.225	75.307	100.561
42	South Africa	37.138	43.334	46.157	59.396	75.275	71.811	78.561	99.005
43	Czech Republic	34.893	45.241	46.453	57.180	76.043	83.088	89.245	95.396
44	Taiwan	53.440	55.500	87.050	93.060	97.850	93.090	75.300	91.410
45	Chile	42.790	43.774	45.446	48.052	56,443	64.768	72.991	86.738
46	Saudi Arabia	39.160	34.350	36.780	47.390	58.600	75.360	72.770	82.920
47	Malaysia	48.557	52.156	51.981	55.026	61.566	75.292	76.376	82.171
48	Qatar	17.500	18.620	21.130	25.700	33.090	55.790	70.370	71.380
49	Slovakia	18.090	23.764	27.053	32.206	44.309	52.527	65.854	66.439
50	Colombia	36.998	37.911	37.720	38.024	43.675	46.392	53.719	64.723

Source: Wikipedia

For all fifty countries in Table 34, the average annual GDP growth was 3.9 percent and the average annual growth of external debt was 13.2 percent. It follows that the growth of the external debt was 3.4 times faster. It's a race to economic collapse.

12. Examples of Countries

The current economic situation of over-indebted countries is shown in three concrete examples.

Example 1: The USA

Table 35: External Debt of the United States

Year	Amount of external debt (in millions of dollars)	Index
2003	6,946,289	100
2004	8,353,479	120
2005	9,476,403	136
2006	11,204,108	161
2007	13,427,103	193
2008	13,749,570	198
2009	13,767,867	198
2010	14,456,194	208

Increase of Debt in the US (2003–2010)

Figure 6

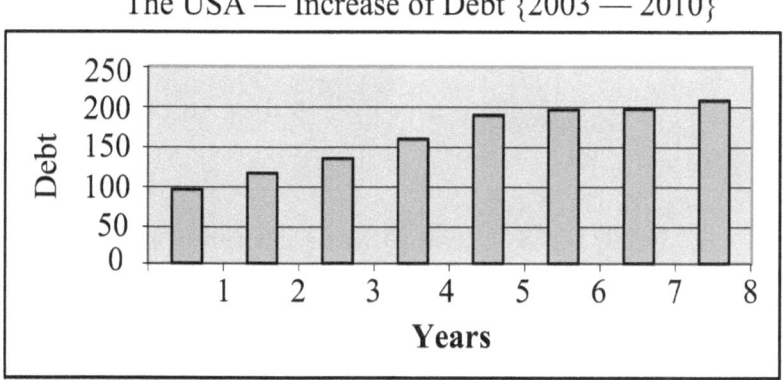

The economy of the United States accounts for about twenty-four percent of the world economy today, and the state of that economy is not good. This can be assessed simply by the degree of indebtedness. The total government debt in February 2014 exceeded $17.290 billion, while the gross domestic product was $16.108 billion. Consequently, the national debt is equal to 107 percent of one year's gross domestic product. At the same time, that debt makes up thirty-three percent of the world's total economic debt. Thus, the indebtedness of the U.S. exceeds the world average to a large extent. This is the first sign of an oncoming economic collapse.

To better understand this, it is useful to observe the tendencies of development of the U.S. debt. In doing so, the economic policies in individual electoral periods should be evaluated:

1. From 1961-1969 during the presidencies of John F. Kennedy and Lyndon Johnson, the American national debt rose from $297 to $385 billion, or 29.6 percent (Democratic Party).
2. From 1969-1977 during the presidencies of Richard Nixon and Gerald Ford, the national debt increased from $385 to $817 billion, or 112.2 percent (Republican Party).
3. From 1977-1981 during Jimmy Carter's presidency, the state debt rose from $817 to $907 billion, or 11.0 percent (Democratic Party).
4. From 1981-1989 during the presidency of Ronald Reagan, the national debt rose from $907 to $2,089 billion, or 130.3 percent (Republican Party).
5. From 1989-1993 during the presidency of George H.W. Bush, the national debt rose from $2,089 to $3,065 billion, or 46.7 percent (Republican Party).
6. From 1993-2001 during the presidency of Bill Clinton, the national debt rose from $3,065 to $5,674 billion, or 85.0 percent (Democratic Party).
7. From 2001-2009 during the presidency of George W. Bush, the national debt rose from $5,674 to $13,768 billion, or 142.7 percent (Republican Party).
8. From 2009-2014 during the presidency of Barack Obama, the state debt rose from $13,768 to $17,290 billion, or 25.6 percent.

The above data show how the American political parties managed the economy and how they contributed to the enormous national debt. When sorting the results according to the two political parties it shows that the Democratic Party increased the debt by 151.1 percent overall. On the other hand, the Republican Party increased the overall debt by 431.9 percent. From this it can be concluded that the Democratic Party managed the increase of government debts of the United States 2.86 times more rationally than the Republican Party. However, it is only a computational that does not take into account the specific political situations in the world.

Table 36: External Debt of the United States

Year	Amount of external debt (in billions of dollars)	Index
1961	297	100
1969	385	130
1977	817	275
1981	907	305
1989	2,089	703
1993	3,065	1,032
2001	5,674	1,910
2009	13,768	4,636
2013	17,200	5,791

Increase of Debt in the US (1961–2013)

Figure 7

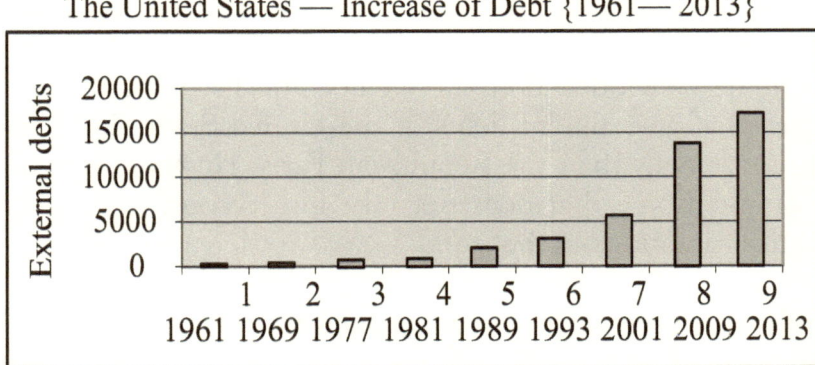

The United States — Increase of Debt {1961— 2013}

Table 36 shows that the average annual growth of the external debt of the United States from 1961 to 2013 was 111 percent. We use the earlier formula to calculate the repayment of such a large debt:

$$G = \frac{D}{B} \; x \; 100 \; x \; T + Y$$

There are two options for the U.S. repayment of government debt.

Variant A:

This variant is based on repaying only that part of the debt that is above the prescribed value of sixty-two percent. The parameters for this variant, taken from the financial tables, are as follows:

- The size of the national debt in the gross domestic product (D) that exceeds the prescribed level of 62% is 107-62 = 45%
- The size of the state budget in the gross domestic product (B) is 38.9%
- The depreciation factor (T) for a period of 30 years and an annual yield of 1% is 0.03874811
- The annual budget deficit (Y) is 0

$$G = \frac{45}{38.9} \times 100 \times 0.03874811 + 0$$

$$G = 1.1568 \times 100 \times 0.03874811$$

$$G = 115.68 \times 0.03874811$$

$$G = 4.48\%$$

If the budget deficit remains at zero, this part of the debt could be repaid in thirty years with an annual growth of the gross domestic product by 4.48 percent. Since a portion of the debt is connected with the deficit in foreign trade, payments will be easier because that part will be repaid by the application of diversified money.

Variant B:

This variant is based on repaying the entire debt amounting to 107 percent of the gross domestic product. The parameters for this variant are as follows:

- The size of the debt of the state budget in the gross domestic product (D) is 107%

- The size of the state budget in the gross domestic product (B) is 38.9%
- The depreciation factor (T) for a period of 100 years and an annual yield of 1% is 0.01586574
- The annual budget deficit is (Y) 0.

$$G = \frac{107}{38.9} \times 0.01586574 + 0$$

$$G = 2.7506 \times 100 \times 0.01586574 + 0$$

$$G = 275.06 \times 0.01586574$$

$$G = 4.36\%$$

If the budget deficit remains at zero, this part of the debt could be repaid in 100 years with an annual growth of the gross domestic product by 4.36 percent. Based on the data on the average growth of the U.S. gross domestic product over the last 223 years of 3.8 percent, it can be concluded that the necessary growth rate of 4.36 percent cannot be realized, and this debt will enter the category of eternal debt.

The Current Trends in the Economic Policy of the United States

On October 17, 2013, after sixteen days of negotiations, the Republican and the Democratic parties in the United States Congress agreed to raise the level of the government's indebtedness for the 2014 fiscal year. In doing so they ensured that government departments and institutions would function normally until January 15, 2014. The technical bankruptcy of the state budget was avoided, but it also raised U.S. debt to the highest level in history. The consequences of the U.S. debt problem were manifested in the slowing of economic growth and the loss of nearly 120,000 jobs.

The American economy is going through its most difficult period in the country's history. People who do not have complete insight into the functioning of multi-economics even foresee the need for a new war to create conditions for an economic boom. This is sheer nonsense. The U.S. economy needs to introduce the principle of economic duals and diversified money. By doing so, by the logic of economic regularities, the country's economy will begin to recover and grow. While the average economic growth over the past 223 years is 3.8 percent, from 2000–10 it was just 1.9 percent. That is the second worst decade in the country's history. The first such period was from 1790–1800.

The current economic deviation rose from a transfer of part of the country's production into less developed states. This can be successfully repaired by appropriate economic policies. Many blame the policies of President Barack Obama for the current economic deviation. That is totally wrong. The condition is the result of U.S. policy over the last forty years, especially after Jimmy Carter left office in 1980, and the beginning of the liberal policy of moving part of the country's production of goods to foreign countries. The American concept of a completely free economy without the need for economic balance carries a devastating virus of economic deviations. Again, the remedy is to put economic duals and diversified money into the economic system. The application of these two concepts protects both entrepreneurs and the state from deviations.

Framework for the Future Economic Policy of the U.S.

If President Obama and his successor wish to avoid the economic collapse of the United States they will have to offer a new framework for the country's economy. This policy should have the following components:

1. The annual budget must be balanced
2. Propose the adoption of austerity programs
3. Prohibit successive lending to the government budget
4. Accurately plan the state budget to account for variations resulting in unexpected expenses
5. Grow the gross domestic product by at least 4.36 percent per annum
6. Good application of economic duals
7. Balance foreign trade operations by rigorous application of diversified money
8. Establish a financial reserve fund.
9. The president should introduce a policy of fighting for rationalization in the state economy to his political party without offering new social benefits in election campaigns

President Obama and his successor will have historic roles in the U.S. Moreover, they will help the entire world economy move toward austerity, affect the world monetary system, and help politicians adopt a more responsible attitude toward the economies in their countries. Adopting the above policies would make it possible for the U.S. to successfully repay its entire foreign debt within twenty years.

Example 2: The United Kingdom

Table 37: External Debt of the United Kingdom

Year	Amount of debt (in millions of dollars)	Index
2003	5,406.413	100
2004	6,729.484	124
2005	7,385.985	137
2006	9,239.287	171
2007	11,260.597	208
2008	9,106.737	168
2009	9,337.345	173
2010	9,554.857	177

Increase of Debt United Kingdom (2003-2010)

Figure 8

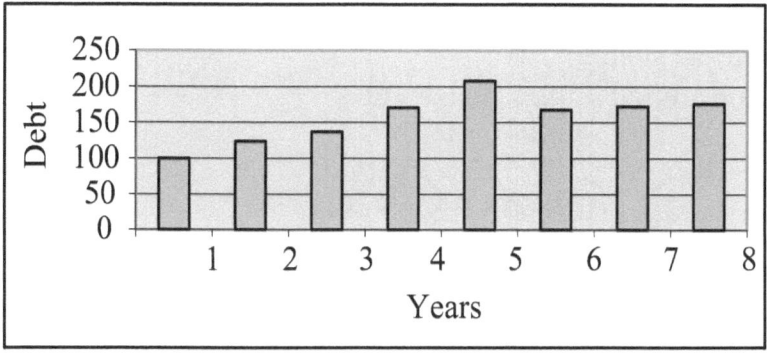

United Kingdom — Increase of Dept {2003 — 2010}

The United Kingdom is the world's second largest foreign debtor. Total government debt at the end of 2010 amounted to $9.555 billion US, which is 91 percent of the gross domestic product. The UK must repay this debt. There are two options for repayment of the UK's government debt. To calculate the repayment capability of repaying this debt, we use the same formula as the U.S. model:

$$G = \frac{D}{B} \times 100 \times T + Y$$

Variant A:

This variant is based on repaying only that part of the debt that is above the prescribed value of 60 percent recommended by the EU. The parameters for this variant are as follows:

- The size of the state budget debt in the gross domestic product (D) that exceeds the recommended height of 60% is 91-60 = 31%
- The size of the state budget in the gross domestic product (B) is 38.9%
- The depreciation factor (T) for a period of 20 years and an annual yield of 1% is 0.05541531
- The annual budget deficit (Y) is 0

$$G = \frac{31}{38.9} \times 0.05541531 \times 100 + 0$$

$$G = 0.7969 \times 100 \times 0.05541531 + 0$$

G = 79.69 x 0.05541531

G = 4.42 %

So, this part of the debt could be repaid in twenty years with an annual growth of the gross domestic product by 4.42 percent. Since part of the debt is connected to the deficit in foreign trade, the payments will be easier because that part will be repaid by the application of diversified money.

Variant B:

This variant is based on repaying the entire amount of debt in the amount of 91 percent of the gross domestic product. The parameters for this variant are as follows:

- The size of the state budget debt in the gross domestic product (D) is 91%
- The size of the state budget in the gross domestic product (B) is 38.9%
- The depreciation factor (T) for a period of 100 years and an annual yield of 1% is 0.01586574
- The annual budget deficit (Y) is 0

$$G = \frac{91}{38.9} \times 0.01586574 \times 100 + 0$$

G = 2.3393 x 100 x 0.01586574 + 0

G = 233.93 x 0.01586574

G = 3.71 %

If the budget deficit remains at zero, this debt could be repaid within 100 years with an annual growth of the gross domestic product by 3.71 if all budget revenues resulting from an increase are used to pay off the national debt.

The Framework for Economic Policy of the UK in the New Election Period

In the new election period in the UK and the EU in 2014, a new economic policy will need to be created if the goal is to reduce the risk of economic collapse in the EU. In this context, the UK will also need to offer a new framework its own economic policies. This policy should have the following components:

1. The annual budget must be balanced
2. Propose the adoption of national austerity programs
3. Prohibit successive lending to the government budget
4. Accurately plan the state budget to account for variations resulting in unexpected expenses
5. Grow the gross domestic product of at least 3.71 percent per annum
6. Apply the principle of economic duals
7. Balance foreign trade operations by rigorous application of diversified money
8. Establish a financial reserve fund

The achievement of such economic parameters will not be politically easy because there will be the need to reduce many social programs, but such a policy would provide the opportunity for the UK to successfully repay the entire foreign debt. With the application of economic postulates, the principle of economic duals, and diversified money, the United Kingdom can successfully repay its external debt as a whole in about ten years.

Example 3: Croatia

Table 38: External Debt of Croatia (2003-2010)

Year	Amount of foreign debt (in millions of euros)	Index
1	2	3
2003	18,727	100
2004	22,933	122
2005	25,761	138
2006	29,273	156
2007	32,929	176
2998	39,124	209
2009	43,117	230
2010	45,860	249

Croatia – Increase of Debt (2003-2010)

Figure 9

Croatia — Increase of Dept {2003 — 2010}

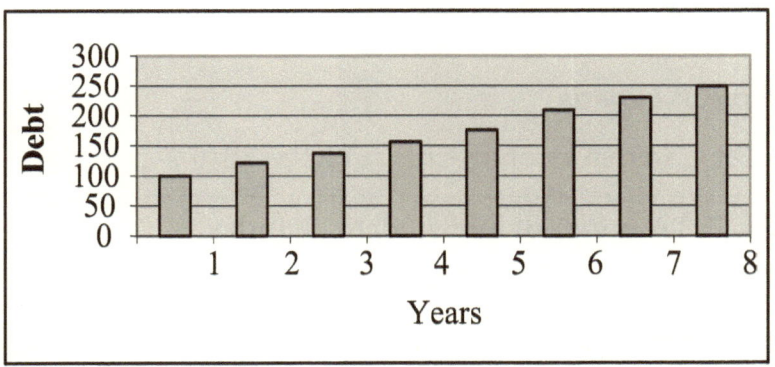

Table 39: External Debt of Croatia (1999-2013)

Year	Amount of foreign debt (in millions of euros)	Index
1999	10,175	100
2000	12,264	121
2001	13,609	138
2002	15,144	149
2003	19,884	195
2004	22,933	225
2005	25,761	253
2006	29,274	288
2007	32,929	364
2998	39,125	385
2009	43,117	424

Year	Amount of foreign debt (in millions of euros)	Index
2010	45,860	451
2011	45,733	449
2012	47,410	466
2013	51,850	510

Increase of Debt Croatia (1999-2013)

Figure 10

Croatia — Increase of Dept {1999 — 2013}

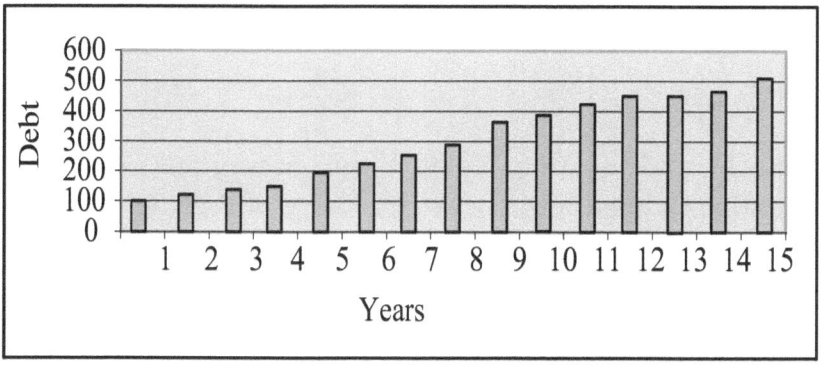

Croatia is a relatively small world debtor. Its foreign debt at the beginning of the year 2013 was 56 percent of the gross domestic product. The state must still repay this debt. To calculate the repayment, we use the same formula as the U.S. and UK models:

$$G = \frac{D}{B} \times 100 \times T + Y$$

The parameters for this variant are as follows:

- The size of the debt of the state budget in the gross domestic product (D) is 56%
- The size of the state budget in the gross domestic product (B) is 38%
- The depreciation factor (T) for a period of 20 years and an annual yield of 3% is 0.06721571
- The annual budget deficit (Y) is 0

$$G = \frac{56}{38} \times 0.06721571 \times 100 + 0$$

$$G = 1.4737 \times 100 \times 0.06721571 + 0$$

$$G = 147.37 \times 0.06721571$$

$$G = 9.91 \ \%$$

This debt could be fully repaid within twenty years if the gross domestic product increases by an average of 9.91 percent. Since about one half of the debt is related to a deficit in foreign trade, it will be possible to repay it by using diversified money. Thus, only the central government debt of fifteen percent of the gross domestic product should be repaid. In this case, the repayment calculation would be changed to a period of ten years and would look like this:

$$G = \frac{15}{38} \times 0.11723051 \times 100 + 0$$

$$G = 0.3947 \times 100 \times 0.11723051 + 0$$

G = 39.47 x 0.11723051

G = 4.62 %

The Framework for Economic Policy of Croatia in the New Election Period

In the new election period in 2014 Croatia too will have to offer a new framework for the state's economy. This new framework should have the following components:

1. The annual state budget must be balanced
2. Propose the adoption of national austerity programs
3. Prohibit successive lending to the government budget
4. Accurately plan the state budget to account for variations resulting in unexpected expenses
5. Have an annual growth in the gross domestic product of 4-4.5%
6. Apply the principle of economic duals
7. Balance foreign trade operations by rigorous application of diversified money
8. Establish a financial reserve fund

As in the U.S. and UK, the achievement of such economic parameters will not be politically easy because there will be the need to reduce many social programs.

Chapter 4

Sources of Danger of Economic Collapse

13. Economic Policy and Debts

In 2014 there are 194 economic areas in the world. These are 194 economic partners who have been convicted to mutual economic cooperation. Statistics show that a small number of these are the so-called economic aristocracy; a greater number are more or less in economic poverty. So, the world economy is divided. The same was also the case in ancient Rome (*Populi Latini* and *Populi Peregrini*).

The economic aristocracy tries to live mainly by using the labor of the poor. For this reason, a large part of the manufacturing industry moved into poor economic areas, which now have to work hard and deliver the produced goods to the economic aristocracy. This economic aristocracy takes over the produced commodity, and pays for them, in a large part, with government bonds, all of which could be bought in five- to ten-year terms. It is the paradigm of the modern economy. At the end of such logic follows an economic collapse, from which a more-realistic economic order will be generated. The Roman, Ottoman, and Chinese empires all collapsed using such logic.

Now is the last moment to seriously change the economic practices of all those living on debts. There is currently a latent financial collapse in the United States and European Union that, left uncontrolled, could explode and produce a global economic deviation of unprecedented proportions. During the last twenty years, the policies in these countries led to social consumption realized by the state budgets going into debt. The politicians in these countries were not engaged in politics of rational consumption, but competed in offering social benefits.

It is justified to ask the question of whether it was the fault of the politicians that had a lack of knowledge of the country's economy, or if the profession failed to provide a sound basis for economic decisions. Now is the time to intensively search for a solution to this complex problem. This solution should be approached gradually in several phases and should be based on the principles of reducing government debt. The multiple stages to the solution would be:

1. The adoption of a balanced state budget
2. The prohibition of successive lending to government budgets
3. Raising the gross domestic product by applying economic duals
4. Elimination of external debt by using diversified money in foreign trade
5. The establishment of off-budget funds for financial reserves
6. Political parties must introduce a policy of fighting for the rationalization of the economy

After the introduction of the above guidelines for the state economy, government loans will begin to gradually decrease, and after a certain number of years will reach the level where it will be possible to manage them rationally.

14. The Budget Deficit of the State

The state budget is the main regulator of the country's economic system. If there is economic abuse or degradation, the state system will behave deviant. Linear practicing of the so-called small budget deficit can always degenerate into a large economic deviation. This deficit can be realized only under certain economic assumptions. The first would be that it must not be introduced in advance, but retroactively. That means that if there was an aggregate percentage increase in the gross domestic product in a year resulting in an excess in the state budget, then only in the next year could the gross budgetary expenditure be increased by that percentage. Translated, this means to spend what was realized. Spending in advance calls an old hunting saying to mind: "Instead of shooting the wild boar, shoot in its shadow."

The second assumption is that the percentage of the gross budget deficit must not be higher than the percentage of annual inflation in the previous year. Some politicians and trade unionists like to say that thrift slows down progress. Aimlessly placing more money in an economic area does not mean also raising labor productivity, improving production technologies, greater rationality, and therefore more resources for consumption. Money is just a mirror image of what is happening in reality. A mirror can become blurred, but that does not mean that reality has changed because of it. It has only become less visible.

15. Successive Granting of Credits to the State Budget

State budgets become insolvent because of inaccurate or manipulative planning of the dynamics of incoming and outgoing cash. This also can happen because of various unpredictable political changes in the world. When the outstanding obligations of the state budget cannot be properly settled the finance minister solves the problem by issuing government bonds and creating debt. This can also happen in case the repayment of credit installments for earlier debt. Then the successive granting of credit begins. That can continue for years and degenerate into a state of eternal debt, the most dangerous debt in a state budget. Such is now the case in several countries, most notably in the United States. Successive long-term lending is detrimental and, in principle, should be illegal.

16. The Deficit of Foreign Trade

The United States is an obvious example of the emergence of economic deviations in foreign trade in the last ten years. The U.S. was an advocate of complete freedom of entrepreneurship. This freedom is useful for the entrepreneurs, but in certain conditions it is detrimental to the population and the state. For this reason, this freedom should also have the responsibility of giving quality to the citizens and the state. For example, the shifting of production from the U.S. to China, and the import of those products back into the U.S., creates an account deficit of the U.S. to China, thereby creating an economic deviation.

In connection with this arises the problem of economic globalization and multi-nationality. In choosing their policies and the search for optimization, large companies have used the constitution of the economic system very well, making the economic borders passable without paying fees for bypassing the economic sovereignty of the states. This is useful for the balance sheets of the companies and they benefit by having to pay no taxes for removing capital from the U.S., and the burden of its current account deficit is transmitted to the state. The goods that are produced abroad are consumable, so when they return to the U.S. it means a benefit for the consumers in the form of lower prices, and for the owners of the companies in increased profits.

However, these same consumers in the U.S., by having the production moved to China, are losing jobs, and the state loses tax income and increases its costs for the unemployed. The balance of that has not been established. According to a rough estimate, the costs of this are considerably higher than the benefits achieved. In addition, when the owners of capital repatriate their financial gains, it is placed mainly in consumption. Such developments create an economic deviation in the form of reducing the growth of gross domestic product in the U.S., reducing the purchasing power of the less wealthy population, and increasing the economic disintegration of the total population. This deviation can be neutralized by applying the principle of economic duals and diversified money. Such economic multi-nationality and globalization is fundamentally detrimental to the United States.

Chapter 5

Protection from an Economic Collapse

17. Conceptually Approaching the Danger of an Economic Collapse

The economic collapse of a state carries enormous economic and political consequences, so the reader of this text will not mind a bit of an allegorical approach to the problem. This refers to the description of various absurdities as solutions to this problem, such as "We do not need austerity policies." This absurdity could be compared with a joke. A bear was constantly hungry so he decided to go to the owl, known as a smart animal, to ask her for advice on how to solve his problem. The owl listened carefully and then said to him, "Bear, turn into a mouse, and you'll have plenty of food." Happy and deeply grateful for the wise owl's advice, he went home. After some hundred meters he remembered that the owl did not tell him how to turn into a mouse. He returned to the owl and said, "Owl, I'm sorry, but you did not tell me how to turn into a mouse." The owl looked at him wisely and said, "You fool, I'm giving you a systemic solution and you are bothering me with technical details!" One often hears similar things from politicians when they talk about the solutions to economic problems.

To solve this problem someone needs to have elementary bookkeeping skills and a little knowledge of what a debt is. When a debtor comes to a state of financial deadlock, economic exhaustion, and is approaching an economic breakdown, he goes into the state of economic collapse. Medicine starts the urgent reanimation of a collapsed person to save his life. It is the same with the economics of a country. A state cannot be liquidated by bankruptcy like a company. It must be economically restored. The only question is how to do it. It stands to reason that the state loses some elements of its economic sovereignty and is forced to endure "humiliation" on the way to rational economic behavior.

18. Concrete Debt Situation

The indebtedness of the two great world economic spaces, the U.S. and the EU, is large and is still increasing. At first glance it can be concluded that it is a threat to the entire world's economy. This danger must be specifically analyzed to reach more conclusions. Therefore, these two economic spaces will also be the subject of further analysis. This is done primarily because these two economic areas have 46.8 percent of the world economy under their sovereignty, and their situation affects the economic situation of the entire world economy.

19. Application of the Principles of Economic Duals

The debts of the state budget can be consolidated in three ways—a drastic reduction of consumption expenditures, quickly and significantly raising the growth rate of the gross domestic product, and a combination of the first two methods. The third way is the most acceptable both economically and politically for the whole economic system. First, the debts of the state budget were created as a result of bad state policies, or as a result of the misapplication of the correct state policies.

A national proverb says "Politicians are sometimes willing to slaughter an ox to get one steak." Raising the gross domestic product, and through it decreasing the indebtedness of the state budget, can be successfully achieved by applying the principles of economic duals. By doing so, two major benefits can be achieved:

1. The production of material products can achieve about forty-three times more economic effects than the production of services.
2. By speeding up payments into the production cycles, economic effects can be obtained which are up to 252 times greater than the slow and anarchic payment.

Therefore, the state which rationally uses this principle will achieve two major economic benefits in the growth of the gross domestic product.

20. Application of the Category of Diversified Money

The basic function of introducing the function of diversified money is, in conditions of free international trade, to interrupt the emergence of foreign debt to one of the partner countries. In addition, it successively contributes to the reduction of already generated debt. Free international trade was a good idea, but it was conceptually incomplete and, as a result, incorrectly applied. The migration of manufacturing activities from the most developed countries into the less developed has a damaging effect to the most developed for several reasons:

1. By moving manufacturing companies overseas, jobs are lost and unemployment is generated, as well as personal strain, problems, and harm to individual people.
2. Tax bases are reduced for the state, thereby reducing total revenue.
3. The costs for the unemployed and their re-employment are increased for the state.
4. The need for professional education in sectors that have moved their production overseas is reduced.
5. Importation of products from companies that have moved their production overseas generates a huge foreign trade deficit.

To eliminate the above-mentioned negative consequences, the government should introduce diversified money in the area of foreign trade as previously described. Specific positive effects of doing so include:

1. Stopping the emigration of production outside of a state and effecting their gradual return.
2. Increase of the number of employees.
3. Increase of the gross domestic product.
4. Increase of total public purchasing power.
5. Greater investments into the rationalization and modernization of production technology.
6. Less avoiding of tax payments.
7. Better understanding of the economic policy by the citizens.

8. Reducing state consumption to rational limits.
9. Help for political parties to form their election economic platforms more easily, usefully, and coherently.

Such effects would contribute to the progress of the state.

21. Establishment of State Financial Reserves

It has been said that to release the budget from various risks arising from unforeseen circumstances the state should establish a special fund of financial reserves. Payments from this fund should be managed by the government, with individual prior approval of the Parliament or Congress. This is necessary to prevent that the fund from degenerating into an illegal credit fund, or possible manipulation and speculations.

22. Improvement of Political Party Programs

Political parties are a platform for a variety of ideas, even those that are highly irrational and meaningless. Two of these parties are important. The first is the one that advocates a position and interest in processing by capital, and the other is one that advocates the position and interests in processing by labor. These are the two poles of a common task and a successful state economy. The quality and importance of the work of these parties is incorporated into the manufacturing processes in the form of taxes and contributions, thus affecting its rationality and competitiveness, the rationality of monetary and financial processes, and improving the state economy as a whole.

The state cannot have a good economy if these two political parties do not perform their functions in a positive way.

Therefore, it is necessary that the professional potential of these parties is at the required height and that it constantly rises. This is particularly important for the function of a good opposition. Often the opposition is subjected to ordinary insults, obscenities, and demagoguery. There is also often no goodwill, sufficient expertise, research, positive conclusions, and inventiveness in the function of the political opposition. The role of politicians in a country's economy should be constructive, not destructive, to the economic success of the state. Ruling politicians logically show the good side of some decisions they want to make, and the job of the opposition politicians is to find and explain the weak or harmful side of that decision. Thus we get a set of good and bad sides of a proposed decision. Thus the analysis becomes complete and then these are the premises for a conclusion. If the advantages of such a decision are in the majority, then it should be adopted and vice versa: if they are in the minority, then it should be rejected. All politicians are needed for making good decisions, if they act in good faith. Opposing is a useful method of logic in researches.

When we talk about the concept of politics it refers to the objectives and procedures used to reach those objectives. Politics should be the medium through which optimal conditions are created for the flourishing of the state's economy. Such conditions are created gradually. Politics in the economics of the country should derive its activity from the principle of economic micro-duals. If this is done, optimal conditions can be achieved in four areas:

- The value of the gross domestic product
- The population's employment rate
- The rate of profits

- The coverage of imports by exports.

In order to obtain these four optimums, it is necessary that the policies positively regulate five economic areas:

- The support of the research of major markets
- The support of the development of production technologies
- The legal regulation of the single payment deadline
- The legal regulation of crediting activities
- The balance of international economic relations.

22.1 Support for the Analysis of Major Markets

The prerequisite for the commencement of any business is the knowledge of supply and demand in general, individual, or segmented markets. Small economic units decay in great numbers because they base their business on a poor assessment of current market conditions. The result of such errors is failure and ruin. There are two main ways companies structure their economic strategy. The first group includes those who depend on the ability of the economic subject, and the second group includes those who depend on the policies and practices of the state.

To minimize the risks of business failure, the state should have a public economic market research institute to provide precise information on relevant markets to entrepreneurs, either free of charge or for a small fee. Diplomatic and consular services of the ministry of foreign affairs, the ministry of economics, and the chamber of commerce should all be connected by such an institute. By doing so, the competence and synergistic efforts of all the protagonists in the preparation and conclusion of economic affairs would be centralized. This would avoid the costly and ineffective "running in place" of politicians and businessmen. It would be known exactly when and where a politician is travelling, what business can be concluded in that country, and who should get the business to assure it was accomplished successfully. In addition, it would also be known exactly what import business could be offered and successfully realized to that country. Finally, it would be known what economic effects the proposed business would bring to both countries. Current practice shows that there are many oversights and errors in this area that produce foreign debts, a violated market with imported products of poor quality, and the destruction of the capacities of domestic economic micro-duals.

22.2 Support of the Development of Production Technology

Considering that the production of material goods and services is the main source of supply in the market and that it creates the purchasing power in the country, it should be technologically developed enough to achieve the quality of the competition in the markets. The technical means, production processes, and organization need to be at or above the average level of the technologically advanced states. This requires different technical skills, research, and application in practice. Maintaining the current level of technological production is an expensive process that only large companies can afford. Small companies must have the possibility of free access to new technological developments. This can be achieved through free professional education and organized technological research in selected areas. A good knowledge of the market is of no use if quality products with competitive costs and selling prices cannot be produced. To achieve easier access, there should be a center for technological information at the state level that would guide interested people to resources for specific areas of knowledge.

22.3 Legal Regulation of the Single Term of Payment

To make the state economic system effective and protect the rights of businesses in the market, the state should stipulate the general terms of payment of contractual and legal obligations. This period can range from ten to ninety days. The longer it is, the less the chance of success a business has, as that term is an element of the economic micro-dual cycle that predetermines success. The results of long-term payments are higher interest costs, higher inventories, and smaller economic fruits. Failure to comply with the defined time limits should be considered economic fraud.

22.4 Legal Regulation of Credit

The prohibition of granting credit for supplies and services is particularly significant. This practice shows that it creates the conditions for insolvency in economic micro-duals. This happens because customers ask the suppliers of products or services to grant them interest-free credit for the maximum period of ninety days, after which they often voluntarily extend that period to 360 days. At the same time, they pay dividends and buy shares in other companies or lend the excess of money at high interest rates with the retained funds. The suppliers tacitly tolerate this for fear of losing a customer. This slows the flow of economic activity in the system and generates a deviation in the economic micro-duals. This market behavior is often the reason for the bankruptcy of businesses that otherwise, by any other criteria, have the general properties necessary for success.

The right of granting credit for regular business operations should be permitted only through the banking mechanism. It could also be permitted to those economic entities that, in addition to their basic business, have the registered activity of financing sales of their products and services. In this case, the volume of credit could not be greater than the volume of funds provided for that purpose in a special account with a commercial bank. Thus, the economic subjects that represent a danger for the normal function of the system would be eliminated from the state economic system. Financing the sale of products or services without insured deposits in a separate account should be regarded as illegal.

It should also be prescribed by law that every economic actor is obliged to monitor his business operations to spot potential danger in time before failing to pay his obligations. If there is such a danger, he must immediately make an assessment of any reserves that will eliminate such a threat. If there are no such reserves, he should ask for credit or remedial help. The business that cannot secure such assistance should report bankruptcy. It should be a legal obligation, and anyone who violates this obligation should be considered as endangering the economic system of the state. It should also be stipulated that each company be required to establish financial reserves in the amount of the liquidity risk. The state government should apply the same legal provisions, with the same consequences, for the person responsible.

22.5 Balancing the Economic Relations Between States

The state should establish a system which provides the financial balance of imports and exports with each country that is an international trading partner. As a rule, import and export should be free according to international agreements, but the importers should diversify money for the imports from individual countries. This would ensure that imports do not exceed the value of exports. These funds should be bought through the banks. The price of these funds would be determined according to their supply and demand. By doing so, all exporters and importers could operate successfully and no specific protectionist measures or currency depreciation would be needed. This is necessary because the international debt on export payments is a source of economic deviations and an unnecessary exploitation of the countries with weaker trade positions. The exploitation is that the state with the stronger commercial position, free of charge, exploits the market of the weaker state and exhausts its financial resources. By balancing the economic damage caused by imports and the economic benefits of exports, justice in international trade is established. Freedom of exports and imports should not provide benefits for only one side. The principles need to be beneficial for both trading parties.

22.6 Regulation of State Entrepreneurship

In principle, the state should not be an economic entrepreneur. However, if there is a need for the development of the state economy, and the state in this case becomes an independent or predominant investor of capital in some economic project, then there must be a separate procedure for the implementation of such activity.

Before the beginning of the investment, a business plan must be made that contains a complete scenario for all activities. In such a plan, the project should have its own economics and must be approved by the representative body of the state. With that business plan, a special government decree should be made that will protect the project from potential corruption of individuals, interest groups, politicians, and political parties. The data concerning the implementation, monitoring, and auditing of such projects have to be fully presented to the representative body and made available to the public.

22.7 Measuring the Economic Success of the State

In order for the state to evaluate its policy in the service of the economy, it should establish indicators of its economic success. It is possible to show this success of the country mathematically. The formula for the calculation of such an indicator is:

$$R = \frac{W \times Sh \times C}{ER}$$

Where:

(R) = the resultant economic performance
(W) = the average net wage
(Sh) = the share of employees in the total population
(C) = the coefficient of imports covered by exports
(ER) = the current exchange rate

This calculation is a good foundation for concrete political decisions in the state economy. This can be seen from the examples which follow. The calculation of this data for Croatia are as follows:

- Average net salary is 5,295 kunas
- The share of employees in the total population is 0.32
- The coverage of imports of goods by the exports of goods is 0.49

- The exchange rate is 1 euro = 7.3 kunas

The resulting calculation of the economic success is:

$$R = \frac{5{,}295 \times 0.32 \times 0.49}{7.3} = 114$$

For comparison, let's look at Germany. Its parameters are:

- Average net salary is 2,830 euro
- The share of employees in the total population is 0.40
- The coverage of imports of goods by the exports of goods is 1.10
- The rate of exchange is 1.00

The calculation is as follows:

$$R = \frac{2{,}830 \times 0.40 \times 1.10}{1.00} = 1245$$

The resultant of the economic success of Germany in 2009 is 1,245. This is approximately eleven times greater than the resultant of the economic success in Croatia, but it may not be equal to the level of economic development. When comparing just the level of economic development of the two countries the difference would be much smaller. The data from this comparison show that Croatia is not economically successful enough.

The estimated parameters for the U.S. are:

- Average net salary was $4,171
- The share of employees in the total population was 0.40
- The coverage of imports by goods for export was 0.62
- Exchange rate is 1.353

The calculation is as follows:

$$R = \frac{4.171 \times 0.40 \times 0.62}{1,353} = 765$$

The resultant economic success for the U.S. in the year 2011 was 765. It was only 0.61 when compared with Germany. If the U.S. had coverage of imports and exports of 1.00, then the resultant would be:

$$R = \frac{4.171 \times 0.40 \times 1.00}{1,353} = 1233$$

Chapter 6

Characteristics of the Debt Situation

23. Basic Criteria for the Debt Relations

The size and structure of the problem of external debt is shown in the previous sections of this text. From this, the risk of an economic collapse for each state and the world economy can be evaluated by deduction. In a large part of the most important countries in the world the amount of foreign debt is constantly growing. However, the ability to repay these debts is not growing. From this, we can conclude that these debts are being converted into a state of eternal debt that can be a trigger for different policy decisions, because creditor states do not show a willingness to write off these debts. The recent situation in Greece is a case in point.

Another great example are the two world economic leaders, the United States and China. The U.S. is the world's largest debtor and China is the largest creditor. The necessity of balancing their economic relations will lead to global economic shocks. The U.S. market is a major global resource and the source from which all the world's major economies are fed. If the U.S. puts that resource into economic balance with the world it will change the whole global structure of economic relations. It is the sovereign right of the United States, and other parts of the world will have to adapt to it. It will be a conceptual economic challenge for all countries and their leading politicians.

In the beginning, each debtor country will need to make an assessment of potential benefits and damage from the necessary world economic changes. Then it will have to program its political activities in the direction of the transformation of the status quo. From this it will make conclusions about its political tasks, the execution of which will be taken over by the politicians. The creditor states will have to do the same thing.

Foreign economic relations between the states will have to move from the current paradigm of total freedom without responsibility into one of mutual responsibility. This will not be palatable for some states because they have acquired the habit of earning on someone else's carelessness and inequality in international economic relations. The answer to this situation was colonialism in the eighteenth and nineteenth centuries. That was a solution on a low political level, but now a higher-level solution is required. That means to respect the sovereignty of others, understand other people's problems, and respect economic laws and limited economic resources. All this includes the principle of economic duals and the category of diversified money. The idea and time for a single world currency and unlimited trading has not yet come. The differences in world development are still too great.

The current economic system of each debtor country should be transformed into a new state. It is essential for the transformation that several criteria are taken into consideration:

1. Equality in the relationship between debtor and creditor

2. Equivalent of usefulness of economic relations for debtor and creditor
3. Consideration of the specifics of the debtor and the creditor
4. Agreement in dealing with the question of relations between the debtor and the creditor on economic principles.

23.1 Equality of Relations Debtors and Creditors

It is normally the practice that the creditor unilaterally determines relations with the debtor because he feels to be the stronger party. It may be useful to the interests of the creditor, but by doing this he takes a part of the bargaining power from the debtor. This could then degenerate into a deviant mutual relationship. Therefore, it is necessary that both sides approach this relationship with a feeling of equality and respect for the other party.

23.2 Equivalence of Usefulness of Economic Relations of Debtor and Creditor

The economic relationship between debtors and creditors should provide equal benefits to both contract parties. It could happen that a business transfer inflicts possible damage to either the creditor or the debtor. Therefore, the application of equality in the contract benefits is important.

23.3 Consideration of Specific Qualities of Debtors and Creditors

Each debtor and creditor has their own specific qualities. It may be the level of development, the political situation in the country, the amount of government debt, the size of natural resources, area, population, various international circumstances, or some other important factor. With such characteristics and potential burdens states are participating in international economic relations and each of these specific characteristics should be considered.

24. Characteristics of the Current Economic Situation

All countries today are part of international economic relations. Into that they bring along their own economic power and problems. The first characteristic within this framework is the level of indebtedness. The second is the ability to repay their debts from the corpus of their economy. Some countries are completely blocked by their debts, while others have been accumulating large economic reserves. There are two problems with this. The first occurs in the debtor countries as they figure out how to pay off the accepted debts. The second occurs with the creditor on how to charge for their claims. Neither have easy tasks.

If you take the example of Greece, it is clear that it can never repay its debts. There, the creditors have made a huge mistake in approving successive borrowing from such a state. This state has two deviations—credit inversion and the state of eternal debt. One successful financial manager said that the only thing to do is simply write off all Greece's debts and not approve any credit for a long time. One successful financial manager said that the only thing to do was simply write off all debts and not approve any credit for a long time. The only loans that could be approved would have a strong capacity for a reverse effect.

Other examples are the USA and the EU, which contain all the features of the current world economic situation.

Economic failure of these entities will lead the whole world into economic chaos and collapse. Their statesmen and those who create the economic strategy should be aware of this.

25. The Facts of the Existence of Economic Space

When we say economic space we are talking about the state, a union of states, and state sovereignty, which means control over the territory and the independence of such control in relation to external influences or aspirations. An economic space has economic sovereignty. Its features include boundaries, economic power, economic law, legal and economic regimes, money, taxes, contributions, marketplace, and customs. This space is largely independent of outside influences. Inside this area, economic activity takes place according to laws that apply only to this area by using its own money according to the procedures prescribed by the government. In this region, taxes, contributions, and customs duties for maintaining economic sovereignty are paid. The economic space can be more or less consistent with, or similar to, other economic areas. The economic space has its own internal and external security and is gravitationally linked with other spaces.

The existence of economic spaces is an objective fact. It limits economic relations among states. Ignoring this fact brings economic damage to partner countries. Each state has its own economic resources and their use provides adequate benefit. If economic relations among economic spaces are not balanced, then the result is damage to one of them. A good part of the nation's politicians do not respect or understand it properly and this causes economic deviation.

Economic equilibrium is a basic economic rule. Compliance with this rule is a main element of protection against economic collapse.

Chapter 7

A Conceptual New Debt Situation

26. The Conceptual Basis for a New Debt Situation

Transformation from the current state economic situation to a new one is needed. This primarily includes lowering the level of debt in all highly indebted countries, thus reducing the risk of economic chaos and collapse. This task is entrusted to politicians. There is no other force which could be engaged to accomplish this. It resembles removing chestnuts from a fiery furnace with bare hands. The politicians will not accept this task with particular enthusiasm, but the situation has reached the point where there is no other choice. Most politicians have knowledge, methods, and other skills necessary to accomplish it. From this situation a new face and value of politicians will emerge, followed by the introduction of pure, optimal, and established economic relationships between countries. The conceptual basis for this exists in the book *Economic Success of the State: The Principle of Economic Duals and the Category of Diversified Money*. A new economic situation will make it so that economic deviations in the form of credit inversions and eternal debt no longer happen.

27. Required Characteristics of the New Debt Situation

The new economic condition of the state should be characterized by economic stability and the ability to control the situation. This stability should include several properties:

1. Each sovereign state can spend only as much as is produced.
2. Credits for consumption without a retroactive effect cannot be approved.
3. There should be a reliable economic mechanism that ensures equilibrium in the balance of foreign trade.
4. Equilibrium in the balance of income and expenditure in the state budget should be established.
5. A financial reserve fund should be formed.
6. The dynamics of budget expenditures for defense must be specifically controlled, particularly in those countries that ideologically deviate from democratic standards and positive international cooperation. Measures of economic restrictions should be imposed against such countries until they change their deviant practices.

The new economic condition of the state should be conceived in such a way that it is positive for all countries in the partnership. The deviant state should be enforced to respect the normal standards of behavior because it is endangering the world economic system.

28. Politicians as Creators of a New Debt Situation

State politicians must be willing to execute plans to solve the problem of financial over-indebtedness, but not all politicians should be invited to solve it. The first condition is that a politician must have a certain level of knowledge in the field of state economics. It's not the same as the ordinary conduct of affairs in mono-economics. This is the field of multi-economics. Here it is necessary to base political activity on other people's economic research. Every problem has its appropriate specific area of research.

The politicians chosen to attack the problems in the state economy must be of quality and who know what is best for their country and how to achieve it. Some politicians are less prepared for the challenge and the great responsibility, and although they want to make the best of it, they are not always successful. Some simply do not have enough economic knowledge, while others do not have the necessary experience. And of course there is always the group of politicians who do not care about anything but their own welfare, and to whom policy is just a means to realize their personal ambitions.

29. Criteria to Transform the Country's Debt Situation

The transformation of the state's economic situation is a very difficult task, as it will determine the living conditions and the economic existence of millions of people. To politicians with little knowledge, this looks simple and easy. However, it is a complex project with countless possibilities. This process should include:

* Optimization of the state's economic policy.
* Activation of the state's economic resources.
* Preparation of economic projects.
* Optimization of the state's economic impacts.

30. Optimization of the Economic and Debt Policy

Solving the problem of the state debt requires a rational economic policy. Those who deal with this task are expected to solve it in the optimal way. By definition, optimum is the best possible choice of a certain size or structure. The deviations from the optimum are negative and come in the form of the disappearance of resources such as damages, losses, risks, and economic waste. The worst kind of negative difference is economic waste. That becomes something that is irretrievably lost.

If the optimum is designated as C and the deviation from the optimum as x, then the value of the non-optimum is (C – X) or:

$$C > (C - X) \qquad (1)$$

Everyone rational will want x to be zero, or if that is not possible, than have its value as small as possible. The success of this is measured by the optimum quotient K.

$$K = \frac{(C - X)}{C} \qquad (2)$$

It is desirable that K have a value of 1, or as close as possible to that. This is the general formula for the desired solution. It can be achieved in various situations and in different ways. The economic policy of the state offers a variety of solutions. To get to the optimum, it must first be determined what the constants are, and then what the variables are in the calculation of the optimum. Economists often say that it is stable money, a wide supply in the market, purchasing power, employment of the population, and the possibility of financing a variety of common needs.

The economic policy that advocates the interests of capital will request the reduction of all non-productive consumption to save as much capital as possible. The economic policy that advocates the interests of work will request the increase of non-productive consumption to make more work available. The best way to reconcile these interests is to find the economic optimum. In this study, the basis of the rules of economic duals is determined, which are the elements on which the optimum of the economic policy should be based. These are the economic variables that need to be converted into economic constants. The economic constants we shall designate as A (1 ... n), and they are:

A1 - the orientation toward the production of material products.

A2 - the economic activation of natural resources.

A3 - the establishment of the balance of economic satellites.

A4 - the exclusion of the generators of economic deviations.

A5 - the stimulation of economic research.

A6 - the exclusion of the deviation of temporal interstate trading.

A7 - the application of the principles of optimum economics.

The formula for the optimum economic policy of the state (C) is as follows:

$$C = A1 + A2 + A3 + A4 + A5 + A6 + A7 \quad (3)$$

30.1 The Orientation to the Production of Material Products

Within the concept of economic policy it is useful to strengthen the economic micro-duals that produce material products because they have on average forty-three times more impact on the population's employment and the activation of other economic resources than the production of services. The production of material products largely creates and accepts various forms of product innovations, achieves more rationalization, engages more national natural resources, and ensures faster economic development in a country. The production of material products must be specialized enough to be globally competitive and able to be included in the international economy.

It is also useful to adapt the concept of non-productive consumption. In the effort of strengthening the production of material products, it is particularly useful to provide state support to industries with a large number of economic satellites, because that kind of production creates a large number of jobs that increase the advantage of economic duals. The support by the state should not go toward financing losses but to those functions that make the production more rational and technologically competitive. The emphasis on the production of material products contributes most to the strengthening of a state's economic power.

30.2 Economic Activation of Natural Resources

Each country has natural resources that can be the basis for the production of material products. Production based on the national natural resources reduces the dependence on foreign markets, transportation costs and the volume of imports, and provides greater safety in business operations. Croatia has four major natural resources. The first is the size of the territory and economic zone of the Adriatic Sea. The second consists of the agricultural land in Slavonia and Medimurje. The third is the forests, and the fourth, fresh water.

The whole concept of the national economic strategy for the production of material products should be based on those resources. In addition, there is a need to stimulate the inventive and creative part of the population directly related to that production. Further, this chapter will describe how the national economic resources can be economically and rationally activated. The Croatian national resources are generally compatible with the traditional, as well as potentially new, global markets. The big problem in the Croatian economy is that there is a great deviation from the optimum.

30.3 Establishing a Balance in the Economic Satellites

The optimum principle requires balance in the economic satellites to eliminate deviations (X). It has already been described that X can cause two possible deviations. The first is the excessive strengthening of the state economy that can easily cause overproduction, the creation of excessive stock, and insolvency. The second is the excessive impoverishment of the state that contributes to economic and technological backwardness. Croatia has a huge imbalance of economic satellites, and therefore X has a large value. This imbalance is because the economic satellites vary considerably from the optimum. This can be seen in how the share of the economic satellites of consumption in the micro-duals is above those in Slovenia, the Czech Republic, and Austria. Also, the economic macro-duals have a large negative balance. If the state does not begin to balance the economic satellites it will fall into excessive foreign debt that will not be paid off for decades and will limit further economic development, making the country a prisoner of debt.

30.4 Excluding the Generator of Economic Deviations

The economic system of a state may suffer damage if it cannot be precisely determined where the deviations originate. The most common culprits are:

- Excessive consumption based on imports
- Non-competitive domestic production of material products
- Insolvency
- Business losses

The first task is to determine how big the economic impact is from each of these sources and then eliminate them. The negative effects from excessive consumption from imports are eliminated by introducing diversified money. The imports then become more expensive and exports more profitable. The problem of non-competitive material products of domestic production is solved by analyzing the cause and then eliminating them. These reasons could include a poor production technology, poor performance on the market, the absence of government support, or a high price due to small-volume economics. By determining the duration of the economic micro-duals and the ability of the economic cores to be transformed into economic satellites, the causes of insolvency can be precisely determined and adequate support given. Business losses are a major generator of economic deviation. If the companies exporting their products have losses they can be eliminated by introducing diversified money. Otherwise, if they are not exporters, they may quickly go bankrupt and disappear from the economic scene.

30.5 Stimulation of Economic Research

A state that has its economics based on a tentative solution of daily politics should initiate an appropriate program for the stimulation of systematically applied economic research. Such research should include two areas: the markets for material products and the technology for the production of those products. They should result in positive responses to the specific requirements imposed by the economics of a successful state. To be able to achieve success in economic research, a conceptual basis should be established on which this research can be carried out to yield the expected results. Such a concept should be based on an appropriate research infrastructure.

The first domain to be explored is the market for specific material products. Research can be done by institutions that have the necessary expertise. Another part of research is the production technology for specific products. This research is complex because it is dependent on progress in many related disciplines. For example, the production technology of a large ship requires a different level of research than the production of shoes. When the manufacturing industry began the technology was created by apprentices and journeymen. However, in today's age of large-scale industrial production and higher product development, technical engineers and scientists are required.

30.6 Eliminating the Deviation of Interstate Temporal Trading

Temporal interstate trading allows immediate consumption but future payment. Such trade of goods that are for daily consumption is an economic deviation. Successful interstate trading is only possible with goods that form economic cores that will produce material products for future export. Otherwise, the state will have foreign debt it is unable to repay. If the state allows uncontrolled temporal interstate trade it will damage future generations by reducing the disposable income and standard of living.

30.7 Application of the Principle of Optimum Economics

Every state can reach its optimal economic policy if it applies certain principles that correspond to civilization's general achievements. This means that they correspond to the developments in ethics, legal standards, science, culture, and the general criteria for the survival of people. The most important principles of optimum economics are:

- Correct data
- Good intentions
- Objective limitations
- Legal arrangements
- Choosing the best solution.

1. The Principle of Correct Data

The principle of correct data is the initial principle of the optimum. If the state does not have correct economic data it does not have the foundation to make relevant conclusions and decisions. Since the state is a complex legal system, it also functions as a complex economic system. The enterprises operate on the principle of so-called linear economics. It is easy to explain. A company, by the logic of profit maximization, takes actions that are useful for it, but some may be contrary to the economic interests of the state. Import companies are interested in greater import volume, even at the expense of the state balance of payments. When searching for the optimum in a country's economics, and when such a complex system is processed and directed, all actions must be based on accurate, provable, and verifiable data. Errors result in the increase of (x) in the form of (C-x), which means increasing economic damage.

2. The Principle of Good Intentions

Occasionally in general policy there is manipulation of economic data to achieve non-economic goals. Doing this is harmful for the country and that is why the application of the principle of good intentions is needed. Good intentions must be seen from the correlation of the correct data and the objective to be accomplished. Often a goal is requested on the basis of one kind of datum that has no correlative connection with the original data. The lack of good intentions is a departure from the optimum and produces economic damage expressed as (C-x).

3. The Principle of Objective Limitations

The principle of objective limitations is an essential factor in reaching the optimal goal. Take a simple example: there are plans to increase the production of a product by twelve percent per annum, but the capacity of the company is such that it can only achieve an increase of four percent. This is an objective limitation. Objective limitations are always a part of determining the optimum and must be taken into consideration when setting the economic goals. The economics of the country have many such restrictions including the limit of the growth of the gross domestic product, exports, imports, consumption, market size, amount of the available capital, and the economic failure of partner countries. When forming the optimum in state economies, the existing and potential restrictions should be taken into account. These restrictions always limit the objectives.

4. The Principle of Legal Arrangements

The principle of legal arrangement guarantees the security of the rights and interests of all participants in an economic area. This principle is ensured by economic regulations and through a competent, efficient, independent, and responsible legal system. The variables from the aforementioned formula are converted into constants in this principle. The principle is the dam that prevents the fluidity and provision of the general policy from attacking the constants and turning them back into the variables, thus nullifying the legal security in the state's economic policy.

5. Principle of the Choice of the Best Solution

The optimum of the economic policy (C) eliminates the negative factor (X) and thus removes potential economic damage. So, in this case, the optimal quotient is K = 1. A deviation from the optimum of the state economic policy introduces the negative factor (X). This creates a non-optimum condition in the economic policy (C – X) and the quotient of optimality (K) decreases below one.

The formula for the non-optimum condition of the state's economic policy is:

$$C - X = C - X1 - X2 - X3 - X4 - X5 - X6 - X7 \quad (4)$$

Specific negative effects of the non-optimum are:

- Stagnation of business and employment
- Neglect of natural resources
- Growth of the share of the economic satellites of consumption in the economic duals
- An increase in the intensity of primary economic deviations
- Inferiority of political decisions
- A steady growth of the state indebtedness
- Maintaining a high level of corruption
- Social dissatisfaction of the population
- Stagnation or reduction of the gross domestic product

The results of the positive effects of the optimum are economic growth and the development of the country, while the results of the negative effects are the stagnation and decline of the state. This can be seen in Tables 40 and 41.

Table 40: Converting the Optimum into the Non-optimum

	A1	A2	A3	A4	A5	A6	A7	A
C	1	1	1	1	1	1	1	7
C-X1	0	1	1	1	1	1	1	6
C-X2	0	0	1	1	1	1	1	5
C-X3	0	0	0	1	1	1	1	4
C-X4	0	0	0	0	1	1	1	3
C-X5	0	0	0	0	0	1	1	2
C-X6	0	0	0	0	0	0	1	1
C-X7	0	0	0	0	0	0	0	0

Table 41: Movement of the Quotient of Optimization

C-X	A	B	K
C	7	0	1
C-X1	6	1	0.86
C-X2	5	2	0.71
C-X3	4	3	0.57
C-X4	3	4	0.43
C-X5	2	5	0.29
C-X6	1	6	0.14
C-X7	0	7	0

Tables 40 and 41 show the conversion of the optimum into the non-optimum. The first column of tables is the optimum and on the abscissa it includes the cumulation of all the seven constants.

Here the relationship between constants and variables is 7:0, and this is the optimum according to formula three. The second column has one constant less because it turned into a variable, so the ratio of constants to variables is 6:1. In the third column, two constants have been transformed into variables, so there has been a second degree of the reduction of the quotient of the optimality. The growth of the non-optimum continues until the eighth column, i.e., the disaccumulation of all seven constants and cumulation of the variables, or to the seventh degree of the reduction of the quotient of optimality. At this stage the value of the quotient of optimality has reached its minimum according to formula four.

The reversal of the non-optimum has an opposite sequence where the individual variables are converted into constants. When all the variables are converted into constants, the quotient of the optimality gets the value of one, which is the optimum. This is shown in Tables 42 and 43.

Table 42: Converting the Non-optimum into the Optimum

	A1	A2	A3	A4	A5	A6	A7	A
C-X7	0	0	0	0	0	0	0	0
C-X6	1	0	0	0	0	0	0	1
C-X5	1	1	0	0	0	0	0	2
C-X4	1	1	1	0	0	0	0	3
C-X3	1	1	1	1	0	0	0	4
C-X2	1	1	1	1	1	0	0	5
C-X1	1	1	1	1	1	1	0	6
C	1	1	1	1	1	1	1	7

Table 43: Movement of the Quotient of Optimization

C-X	A	B	K
C		7	0
C-X1	1	6	0.14
C-X2	2	5	0.29
C-X3	3	4	0.43
C-X4	4	3	0.57
C-X5	5	2	0.71
C-X6	6	1	0.86
C-X7	7	0	1

The application of the principle of optimum economics starts with the assumption that the economic constants are good and useful solutions, and the economic variables are unstable solutions that cannot be used to accurately determine the economic benefits and a positive influence. The constants produce safety, the variables the opposite. In terms of a complex and difficult economy, like a state's, the existence of economic variables as system solutions is a potential and hidden danger as preconditions for deviation.

The complex economics of the state and the linear economics of companies are not always governed by the same logic. The economics of business administration has only one legitimate interest—to achieve the economic fruit of profit. The economics of the state have a lot of diverse interests and goals that quite often conflict with the interests of individual companies.

31. Activating the Economic Resources of the State

To achieve economic prosperity in a country, a competent economic policy is needed. Such a policy should result from an election campaign. To be able to track the economic progress, the politicians should offer economic projections in their campaigns, by which the movement of economic progress could be accurately monitored. The projection of economic policy is very important and defines the framework of its activities. The absence of such projections creates the circumstance where the effects cannot be controlled. A good and responsible politician would gladly accept the projection of the policy as a measure to assess the effectiveness of his operations. By comparing the indicators of negative variances of the development at the beginning and the end of the electoral mandate, an image is obtained of how successful the policy was and how it contributed to the advance of the development. If there is no success, a deductive analysis can determine in which areas the policy was unsuccessful and the reasons. It is also an objective basis for seeking a new policy mandate and a chance for opponents to legally destroy unsuccessful policies.

Each of the reasons for the policy failures needs to be confirmed through a thorough analysis. There must not be any incompetence in the manner of the opposing politicians. Any error in the treatment and presentation of the problem primarily rests at their feet. To effectively prove his findings, he must be more thoroughly prepared than the ruling politician. A good performance by the opposing politician can force the ruling politician to bring more effort and quality into his work.

Political problem solving usually falls into two categories, traditional and progressive. A progressive politician should always be better than the traditional because he has to overcome two resistances—the natural resistance to the new and unknown by the public, and the greater confidence in the quality of the ruling politicians. To achieve an advantage, the opposing politician needs to dispense more premises for his conclusions, and have a better methodology for the presentation of the topics. He must be a "Renaissance man."

The economic progress of the state must be the most important political goal because it determines the living conditions for the population. For this reason, special attention must be paid and a special strategy developed. It should have a foundation that allows a shift from the current state to a new and better one. To become a reality, its strategy should include the economic resources of production. It is a complex task because a variety of uncertainties are hidden in the future and stand against its realization, the power of which increases proportionally to length of time into the future. This uncertainty is mainly related to the development of technology, wider political changes, natural phenomena, and the social behavior of people. Because of this, politicians must make models of past economic behavior and analyze them. Then an analysis of the historical differences that have occurred can be made. These two premises should be the basis for conclusions. In that way, the knowledge and experience of the past are transferred into the present.

Three elements are important to the economic strategy: the choice of objectives, the selection of economic resources, and the method for the processing of resources. To obtain a valid economic strategy, goals should be realistically set, and the available economic resources and processing technologies known. Each of these elements must be thoroughly investigated from all aspects because failure to do so always results in a half-success or failure.

Economic strategy includes growth and development. The growth is expressed through the quantity of the results, while development is expressed through the quality of the results in terms of improved characteristics, better quality, or increased value. Every economic goal should include quantitative and qualitative aspects.

The first side of the economic micro-dual is the production of economic resources. This production needs to create products that will be accepted in the market, because it is a condition that micro-duals alternately multiply and create economic fruit. This side of the economic micro-dual is very complex and is the base that brings progress to the economic subject and the state. Therefore, it should be given all the creative force necessary. The amount of normal production can be increased rapidly by buying plants, machinery, seedlings, seeds, breeding material, and the like, but quality cannot be increased by any quick or simple procedure. This aspect needs an investment of much more effort. Economic growth increases the number of jobs of equal value and economic development jobs of increasing value. For example, human beings were created and use various experiences and their memory to learn. Multiplication did not make human beings more human, only more numerous. By economic growth, the total wealth of the community is increased in proportion to the number of jobs, and the average individual in that community generally only reproduces his status. Examples of this today are the developing countries where the total volume of the social wealth is growing steadily but the level of individual wealth is changing very slowly.

Economic development in the same measure increases the wealth of the individual and society. Economic development creates a greater volume of average individual income where needs of a higher order are satisfied. Economic strategy is different from policy because it does not prescribe the way to achieve goals, and it differs from the plan in that it has not been obtained by calculation or the calculative basis of some existing process. The economic policy does not use ordinary statistical data. It includes probability, entrepreneurship, research, creativity, community, social capital, and complex indicators yielding results of a higher level.

Economic strategy is conceptually determined and is limited by economic resources, the major one being human knowledge. This is the only resource that increases by use. Economic strategy must bring the economic resources in harmony to facilitate their processing. It has to bring into harmony the knowledge, working, and entrepreneurial skills of the population, research, legislation, services of government bodies, natural areas, commercial and residential premises, raw materials, technologies, energy resources, water and sanitation, roads, communications, markets, and funding. By processing these economic resources, economic progress is produced. The better the processing, the greater the progress.

Economic progress can be measured by several indicators. The main two are the quantitative and qualitative. In principle, economic strategy solves the problems of insufficient resources first. The sequence is as follows: knowledge and ethics of the people, infrastructure, space, research, technology, products, and financing. It creates economic growth and development, which leads to an inversion of the costs. Initial costs are always high—often higher than the revenue generated. Later they fall significantly and the revenue should progressively grow. In the initial period, costs grow for investment in the education of workers, upgrading of infrastructure, research, construction of fixed assets, and purchase of technology. After all these adjustments, the results begin to progressively grow and bring broader benefits.

The economic strategy needs to be rationalized. Its rationalization is executed by the election of objectives where the economic goals are more intensely realized. In order to reach a rational economic strategy, certain research must be already done. The best method for this is modeling, because it is one of the research methods that creates hypothetical situations from a complex set of facts, the processing of which gives some results. By comparing the resulting data of several such models, a basis is formed that can determine which model will bring the best results.

The economic strategy model should determine the economic objectives, the type and volume of surplus resources, determine the balance of surplus and scarce resources, the form of the processing the economic resources, and identify the expected results of that processing. Some of the projected economic strategies are presented as possible models. As a basis for the choice of the optimal model, a number of assumptions and conditions for a rational solution of the problem of economic strategy should be understood. These include the existence of a conceptual basis for rationalizations in the economic strategy, the existence of an object of that rationalization, and the existence of the possibility for the rationalization of the economic strategy in various combinations.

The production for the market supply starts with analyzing incoming resources, both primary and secondary. Primary resources are those created by nature and human labor in the form of products and services; markets are the secondary resources. To perform an economic activity, each produced resource must have an appropriate demand. The production and the market have their own capacities. The task of the economic strategy is to enable a rational exploitation of these capacities.

Each country is a limited economic space where economic activities take place. Production resources can be used rationally or irrationally, be planned or "wild." All the highly developed countries in this age of liberal capitalism have used their natural economic resources wildly; therefore, some have overused them. For this reason, they have needed to activate the natural resources of other countries, mainly those that are less economically developed and therefore had not used up their natural resources.

A state that has a rational economic strategy also has a good economic policy, while a country that does not exists in the wild exploitation of its economic resources, thus significantly limiting its future progress. The main resources for production are the population, the natural space, water, the built space, locations, raw materials, technologies, energy, roads, the market, and financial resources.

32. Preparation of Economic Projects

Economic projects are a type of business activity. They are entrepreneurial projects processed by a legal person, such as an enterprise or corporation. By the development of techniques and technologies, economic projects are constantly processed in a better way and with increased efficiency. The production of material and non-material products in the form of services are increased. By the specialization of production technologies, the mass of specialized products is also increased. The increased mass of specialized products requires a continual increase of the market for their sale. Economic projects differ by the type and quantity of the economic resource that can be processed. Because of this, there are many kinds of economic projects, namely those based on underground sites, agricultural land, forest resources, construction, energy, the use of water, employee-intensive projects, transport, technology, tourism, household services, and education, to name just a few. When a concrete economic entity wants to determine its economic strategy, it should keep in mind what kinds of resources are available to adapt these projects to the appropriate economic resources.

33. Optimization of the Economic Effects of the State

By applying the concept of economic micro-duals, the state can maximize its economic results. This can be done by using the benefits of the duals to achieve the economic optimum. To determine the optimum there must be a sound base. Also, measures must be set to evaluate each model of rationalization. As the basis for the selection of the optimum, a number of assumptions and conditions for a rational solution can be understood. These are primarily the existence of a conceptual basis for the rationalization of state economics by economic micro-duals, the existence of a goal of rationalization, as well as the existence of a rationalization possibility in various forms. Based on these assumptions, the optimal solution can be chosen that is economically advantageous and also socially beneficial. The optimum is found by measuring and evaluating possible solutions. The criteria for this are mainly quantitative and include the length of the duration of the economic micro-duals, the height of the profit in economic satellites, the proportion of reproductive economic satellites in the total structure of satellites, and whether imports are covered by exports.

In further analysis, three forms of rationalization, Models A, B, and C, will be given. In order to see the influence of the micro-dual in particular models of different durations, various shares of the reproductive satellites in the micro-duals will be introduced. The models will be analogous to the economics of the Croatian state. They can be generalized and then applied for any country. These three models are the minimum number of combinations. This number may be higher, depending on the choice of the data. In these models, the results of different combinations of data are abstracted, as well as all the specifics, irregularities, and minor deviations of the individual data values that may affect the process of calculating the results.

1. Assumptions and Conditions for the Formation of Models

To be able to begin the formation of the models in of the economic micro-duals, certain prerequisites are necessary. These assumptions are of technological and marketing natures. The technological assumptions include the economic core area. They should meet the technology in production and consumption. This means that their production should be highly productive, the materials used in the production comply with environmental criteria, the rational business logistics of the finished products are enabled, and that the products meet all the criteria of safe, easy, and enjoyable use.

Market conditions include two aspects. The first is that there is a legal possibility of the free use of resources from a foreign market. This means that the access to compatible markets is possible without payment of special compensation for their use. This issue is related to the status of bilateral and multilateral economic relations. By using the foreign market, the exporting country realizes the economic fruits in the form of profit and keeps the jobs in the chain of multiple economic micro-duals. This can bring many economic benefits. The importing country may require payment of a part of the economic fruits through a variety of forms. For these reasons, the principle of equal economic benefits and harms is applied. That means balancing the value of imports and exports. For example, in Croatia this is especially important in the fields of energy, automobiles, specialized computer equipment, and a variety of technical consumer goods. Therefore, it must form coordinated partnerships with the exporting countries. The crude application of the principles of free markets takes Croatia, as well as any other state, into economic deviation if the interstate trade shows a deficit and the trade is temporal.

Another aspect is whether the products for export are competitive with regard to prices, deliveries, and services. Requirements for the formation of models include the existence of possibilities related to the shortening of the duration of the economic micro-duals in the areas of payments, the share of the reproductive economic satellites in all satellites, the existence of the required number of unemployed people who have the knowledge and ability to accept available jobs, and the ability of the state administration to secure partnerships with other countries to cover imports by exports.

2. Model A

This model of rationalization is based on the assumptions that the average duration of economic micro-duals in the country is reduced from ninety to sixty days, and that in connection with that there are increases in the gross domestic product and number of employees. The result is a reduction in the number of unemployed equivalent to the increase of the gross domestic product, and increased profits in the same proportion. The second assumption is that the proportion of reproductive economic satellites in the micro-duals remains unchanged at 0.35. The increase of production increases the coverage of imports by exports, which is currently about 0.479. In addition, total austerity is increased by the absolute amount that corresponds to the height of the paid salaries for the increased number of employees. Based on these data, the economic effects of rationalization are determined.

The elements to calculate the economic results are as follows:

- Shortening of the duration of the economic micro-duals in the state (S)
- The proportion of reproductive economic satellites (P)
- The annual value of the gross domestic product (GDP)
- The number of employees (E)
- Exports (EX)
- Imports (IM)
- Profit (PR)

The initial data of Croatia for this model are:

- GDP is 47,871 (in million euros)

- The number of employees in the economy is 886,900
- The number of unemployed is 285,800
- The proportion of reproductive economic satellites in economic micro-duals is 0.35
- The shortening of the duration of the economic micro-duals in the state is 0.34
- Imports are 18,879,000 (in million euros)
- Exports are 9,043,000 (in million euros)
- The coverage of imports by exports is 0.479
- Profit is 5,014,000 (in million euros).

(1) The formula to calculate the increase in gross domestic product is:

$$\text{GDP growth} = \text{GDP} \times S \times P \qquad (1)$$

It follows the calculation of growth, which is:

The increase in GDP = 47,871 x 0.35 x 0.34

= 47,871 x 0.119
= 5,693 (in million euros)

In this model, the gross national product would be increased from the current 47,871,000 to 53,564,000, or 11.9 percent.

(2) The formula to calculate the increase in the number of employees is:

$$\text{The increase in the number of employees} = E \times S \times P \qquad (2)$$

It follows the calculation of growth, which is:

The increase in the number of employees = 886,900 x 0.35 x 0.34

$$= 886{,}900 \times 0.119$$
$$= 105{,}541$$

In this model, the number of employees in the economy would be increased from the current 886,900 to 992,441, or 11.9 percent. At the same time, the number of unemployed people would decrease from the current 285,800 to 180,259.

(3) The formula to calculate the increase of the profit in economic satellites:

$$\text{Increase in profit} = PR \times S \times P \qquad (3)$$

The resulting calculation is:

$$\text{Increase in profit} = 5{,}014 \times 0.35 \times 0.34$$
$$= 5{,}014 \times 0.119$$
$$= 597 \text{ (in million euros)}$$

The profit in the economic satellites in this model would be increased from the current 5,014 to 5,611 (in million euros).

(4) The formula for the calculation of the coverage of the import by export:

Increasing EX
The increase of coverage of imports by exports =   (4)
IM

It follows the calculation of the increase of the coverage of import by export, which is:

$$\text{The increase of coverage of imports by exports} = \frac{5{,}693}{18{,}879} = 0{,}302$$

In this model, the coverage of imports by exports has increased from the current 0.479 to 0.781.

3. Model B

In this model of rationalization, the assumption is that the average duration of economic micro-duals in the country is reduced from ninety to forty days, the number of employees is increased, the number of unemployed reduced, and the profit is increased in the same equivalent. Also, the coverage of imports by exports is increased in the absolute amount of the increase of the gross domestic product. Also, total savings are increased by the absolute amount that corresponds to the height of the paid salaries for the increased number of employees. The other economic indicators of the state are not changed. The process of calculating is the same as in Model A.

The data for the calculation in this model of rationalization are:

- GDP is 47,871,000 (in million euros)
- The number of employees is 886,900

- The number of unemployed is 285,800
- The proportion of reproductive economic satellites is 0.35
- The shortening of the duration of the economic micro-duals is 0.44
- Imports are 18,879 (in million euros)
- Exports are 9,043 (in million euros)
- The coverage of imports by exports is 0.479.

The results of the calculation are:

(1) Increase of the GDP = 47,871 x 0.35 x 0.44 = 47.871 x 0.154
= 7.372 (in million euros)

In this model, the gross national product increases from the current 47,871 to 55,243 or 15.4 percent.

(2) The number of employees increases from the current 886,900 to 1,023,483, or 15.4 percent, while unemployment is reduced from 285,800 to 149,217.

(3) The profit in the economic satellites is increased from the current 5,014 to 5,786 (in million euro).

(4) The coverage of imports by exports is increased from the current 0.479 to 0.869.

4. Model C

The assumptions for this model of rationalization are extensive. The average duration of economic micro-duals in the country is reduced from ninety to forty days, and the proportion of reproductive economic satellites is increased from 0.35 to 0.45.

Data for the calculation in this model are:

- GDP is 47,871 (in million euros)
- The number of employees in the economy is 886,900
- The number of unemployed is 285,800
- The proportion of reproductive economic satellites is 0.45
- The shortening of the duration of the economic micro-duals in the state is 0.44
- Imports are 18,879 (in million euros)
- Exports are 9,043 (in million euros)
- Coverage of imports by exports 0.479.

The calculation is:

- The gross domestic product increases from 47,871 to 57,349 (in million euros), or 19.8 percent.
- The number of employees increases from 886,900 to 1,062,506, while unemployment is reduced from 285,800 to 110,194, which is 2.4 percent of the total population.
- The profit in economic satellites is increased from the current 5,014 to 6,007 (in million euros).
- The coverage of the imports by exports moves from the current 0.479 to 1.023.

The exports would be slightly higher than imports, which would be used to pay off the external debt of the state.

5. The Choice of the Optimal Model

In the previous three models, the possibilities of the rationalization of the economics of the country, between which one should be chosen on the basis of quantitative criteria, are shown. This can be done by comparing the results of rationalization models. The optimal model is identified by the highest number of positive results. The comparison is shown in Table 44.

Table 44: Indicators of the Results of the Rationalization (ABC)

Criteria	Model A	Model B	Model C
GDP growth (in million euro)	5.693	7.372	9.478
The increase in the number of employees in economy	105,541	136,583	175,606
The increase in profit (in million euros)	597	772	993
Increase of the coverage of import by export (the quotient)	0.302	0.390	0.502

The data in this table was obtained by computation and are conceptual parameters. The computational procedure has abstracted all the problems that might arise from the specific practices and policies related to the procedure of the realization. Model C showed the best results in all four measured parameters.

6. Testing the Selected Model

Model C, the best of the three, can be tested by two criteria. Shortening of the duration of the economic micro-duals by two days can be chosen as the first criteria, and the second can be the increase of the number of reproductive satellites for one satellite at one-tenth of the economic core. The test result must show whether there is a possibility of increasing the effects. If during the testing the possibility of a further rationalization occurs, then a new scenario for the rationalization, Model D, would be formed that would be more favorable than Model C. In this case, it should be analyzed whether negative consequences could occur when put into practice. These consequences would probably arise only in the first period. They could appear as difficulties in the logistics of acquiring manufacturing components, but these difficulties would encourage rationalizations in the organization of production.

The result of a further shortening of the duration of micro-duals would contribute to the increase of all economic results in Model C by five percent. Increasing the number of reproductive economic satellites in one-tenth of all the micro-duals would bring an increase of all economic effects in Model C by sixty-four percent. In order to practically implement this rationalization, there should be a change in the structure of one-tenth of the economic core by increasing the proportion of the production of more complex material products. This can be done by changing the economic policy of the state. From the above it can be seen that the more favorable Model D could be formed. In this case, the description of this model should be included in the analysis.

Table 45: Indicators of the Results of the Rationalization (ABCD)

Criteria	Model A	Model B	Model C	Model D
GDP growth (in million euros)	5.693	7.372	9.478	16.018
The increase in the number of employees in economy	105,541	136,583	175,606	296,774
The increase in profit (in million euros)	597	772	993	1,678
Quotient of the increase of the coverage of imports by exports	0.302	0.390	0.502	0.848

Table 46: Indicators of the Total Result of the Rationalization

Criteria	Before rationaliza-tion	Model A	Model B	Model C	Model D
GDP (in million euros)	47,871	53,564	55,243	57,349	63,889
The number of employees in economy	886,900	992,441	1,023,483	1,062,506	1,183,674
Profit (in million euros)	5,014	5,611	5,786	6,007	6,692
Quotient of import/ export coverage	0.479	0.781	0.869	0.981	1.327

If the weakest indicator in this table was one point, the second result would be two points, etc. The value of the relationship of these results could then be easily seen. The model that gets the highest total score is the most favorable. This is illustrated in Table 47.

Table 47: Rating the Indicators of the Rationalization

Criteria	Model A	Model B	Model C	Model D
GDP growth	1	2	3	4
The increase in the number of employees in economy	1	2	3	4
The increase in profit	1	2	3	4
Increase of the coverage of imports and exports	1	2	3	4
Total result	**4**	**8**	**12**	**16**

7. The Economic Effects of the Optimal Model

Once the optimal model of rationalization of a country's economy in the field of economic micro-duals is chosen, it is possible to determine the effects that are achieved. The effects are economical and are the result of shortening the duration of the micro-duals from ninety to thirty-eight days, or by 57.8 percent, increasing the proportion of the reproductive economic satellites from 0.35 to 0.45, or by 28.6 percent, and increasing the number of reproductive economic satellites in the micro-duals by one satellite in one-tenth of micro-duals. By doing so, the following would be achieved:

- Increase in gross domestic product by 33.46 percent
- Increase of the number of employees by 33.46 percent

- Increase of the coverage of imports by exports from 0.479 to 1.327

The effects of the optimal models are conceptual. Their realization depends on the creation of assumptions and conditions on which this model is based. Such an increase of economic effects can seriously improve the economics of the country. If the data before and after the rationalization are compared, large positive differences are evident. These can be seen in Table 48.

Table 48: Comparison of the Indicators Before and After the Rationalization

Indicators	Before rationalization	After rationalization
GDP (in million euros)	47,871	63,889
Profit	5,014	6,692
Number of employees in the economy	886,900	1,183,674
Number of unemployed	285,800	-10.974
Import (in million euros)	18,879	18,879
Export (in million euros)	9,043	20,767

The 33.46 percent growth in the GDP in the rationalization of Model D shows progress in the economy of the analyzed state.

Economic fruits are increased in the form of business profits and purchasing power, the number of employees is increased, the number of retirees could be decreased by their re-employment, and state foreign debt can be repaid. Moreover, there are non-analyzed benefits in the form of the complete elimination of the state budget deficit, with the possibility of increasing average pensions. From the data of the tables it can be seen how big and decisive the effect of the rationalization in economic micro-duals is on the economy of the analyzed state.

Chapter 8

Final Comments on Research

The main task of this study was to obtain relevant answers to solve several important problems that exist in the area of debt of developed countries. Many premises were found on the basis of which to derive useful conclusions.

Three main questions were asked in this study: how to stop going further into debt, how to begin to amortize the existing debt, and how to develop a government policy that will realize these goals and prevent a large-scale economic collapse. The objectives of the research were to explain the conceptual framework for the amortization of debts, how to reduce them in an economically realistic framework, to explain the concept of economic deviations of credit inversions and the state of eternal debt, explain the danger of economic collapse, and describe a possible framework for the transformation of the current economic situation into a new one.

In the performed research and the text below, premises are established upon which it is possible to provide answers to the questions in the form of conclusions. These conclusions are:

1. Between 2003-10, the major developed countries of the world entered a high level of indebtedness. This situation was

caused mainly by account deficits in foreign trade. Among these countries, the largest amount of debt is held by the United States. Its external debt entered a state of eternal debt. This debt has also entered into the economic deviation of a credit inversion. Such a situation has the characteristics of high economic deviations.

Other developed countries also entered similar conditions. The total debt of the United States in the mentioned period increased by 108 percent, the UK seventy-seven percent, France 121 percent, Spain 136 percent, Ireland 214 percent, and Australia 179 percent. In Germany, this growth was relatively minimal at only fifty-seven percent. In Croatia, the debt rose 149 percent, among the highest worldwide. It is characteristic that the average debt is steadily growing from year to year. Only the UK has seriously reduced the debt in one year. No other state has stopped or reduced its debt. This cannot last long because it leads to economic collapse.

2. To cover the debt, the states issued government bonds. However, the economic conditions did not allow the repayment of debts, only their successive growth. No state has prepared and published a scenario for the repayment of debt. This is a deviation of economic policy. The publication of such a scenario is a necessity to prevent the state from using force to solve the problem.

3. The repayment of debts will require major economic changes that last for a long time. This will also lead to political changes. The biggest improvement will be realized if diversified money is introduced in foreign trade. Applying these economic methods will cause a reduction in the foreign debts of the state by automatism. On the other hand, the strict application of economic duals will result in an increase in gross domestic product, the economic effect of which will gradually reduce internal debts.

4. The result of excessive indebtedness of states is the emergence of two economic deviations, namely credit inversion and the state of eternal debt. Credit inversion occurs when the benefits of debt start to be less than the damage of the debt. When the debt of a state becomes so large that its rate of repayment cannot be amortized from the economic fruits of the country, and only by establishing new debt, then the debt is considered eternal debt. This is the moment to raise the economic alarm. If this fails, economic collapse occurs that will force the destruction of the former economic system.

5. When the economic collapse occurs, the former strength of the economic corpus is significantly reduced. It then causes the state to solve the economic problems by force. This involves three phases. The first is the restructuring of the economic system to a lower level by annulment of the state budget deficit and by stopping further increased debt. The second phase is to stabilize the economic system at a lower level. The third is a gradual and long-term reduction of the level of indebtedness. According to previous economic experience, that means the return to the economic situation of eight to ten years ago. It also brings secondary effects associated with technological and other developments.

6. The first and most important task in restoring the collapsing economic situation in a country should involve the main political parties and politicians. This is a difficult and challenging task. In such an economic situation, parties and politicians should be very careful not to slow down the recovery of the economic system because of cheap populism and a lack of competence. They must go through their internal catharsis. In this stage, there should be an association between economic knowledge and political pragmatism. Experience shows that political destruction in various forms then becomes stronger.

The government needs a conceptual political opposition in this phase of the economic life, but it must be based on competence and good intentions and not on the opposite concept.

7. If the United States and the European Union do not start to rapidly and rationally solve the problem of indebtedness, the consequence will be an economic collapse of unprecedented size. China will then take over the economic role that the U.S. had after World War II.

8. To overcome the problem of government debts and prevent deviant behavior in the state's economic policy it is necessary to give special attention to the quality of people that will be given the opportunity to manage the economic fate of the country. This requires at least two of several possible conditions.

The first condition is that people with high standards are selected to manage the state affairs. They are characterized by high education, high general culture, strong personal morals, tolerance towards other people, good intentions, kindness, preference surveys in the work they do, high natural intelligence, and respect for others as well as themselves. The second condition is that political figures have the conceptual and theoretical knowledge of the functioning of the state's complex economic system. The lack of these two conditions will certainly lead to the degradation of the state.

Chapter 9

Criteria for Solving the Problem

To be able to come to essential conclusions in connection with money and debts we should remember seventy years ago. After the agreement at the conference in Breton Woods in 1944, the last gold standard came into being, by which a greater number of countries linked the exchange rate of their national currencies to the U.S. dollar. A fixed gold price of $35 per ounce was established and promised. In the middle of 2011 this price was increased to about $1,900, almost fifty-four times more. The average annual increase of the gold price was ninety percent.

The consequences of the Vietnam War forced President Richard Nixon to abolish the Gold Standard in 1971 and the convertibility of the dollar into gold. After that, the ability to issue money in unlimited amounts was created. Money was issued as credit debts. From that time, a stampede of money and debts began to develop. Since then, the U.S. debt has grown at an annual rate of 111 percent, twenty-three percent faster than the price of gold. This also created the average annual nominal increase of wages of 16.6 percent, which can be seen in Table 49.

Then began a game of numbers. The debts of all of the most developed countries turned into eternal debts and generated a credit inversion. A scheme for the gradual recovery of the credit deviation at the state levels is proposed below. For this to work, the state politicians must be fully responsible. They must stop the conceptual economic insufficiency. If they do not, an enormous global economic collapse will occur with the adequate political consequences.

Table 49: Increase of the Average Annual Salary in the United States

Year	Salary
1971	6,497.08
1981	13,773.10
1991	21,811.60
2001	32,921.92
2011	42,979.61

Scheme 4: The State Debt Reduction

		State Budget	Foreign Trade
01	Phase of stoppage the successive growth of debt	* Annulment of the state budget deficit	* Issue of official papers concerning the use of diversified money in foreign trade

		State Budget	Foreign Trade
02	Phase of stabilization of the economics of the state	* Introduction of financial rules regarding the balance of income from production of material products and services on one side, and consumption expenditures on the other (economic duals) * Introduction of the expenditure position for the co-financing of exports to repay the external debts at the level of the difference between the diversified and current exchange rate of the domestic currency	* Start of paying the export and import only by diversified money
03	Phase amortization of debt	* Payment of debts of the state budget according to the plan of repayment	* Repayment of debts by the foreign trade surplus
04	New going into debts	* New going into debts of the state budget can be approved after all earlier debts have been repaid	* A new debt in foreign trade cannot be approved

		State Budget	Foreign Trade
		* New going into debts can be approved to the level of mathematically possible repayment of the debt based on the growth of the domestic gross production	
05	Mathematical upper limits for the state debt	* The total debt of the state budget can be based according to four conditions and in two variants: * First variant: (1) debt level 10% GDP (2) term of repayment of the debt 10 years (3) annual interest rate 3% (4) constant annual growth of GDP 3.1% * Second variant: (1) debt level 30% GDP (2) term of repayment of the debt 30 years (3) annual interest rate 2% (4) constant annual growth of GDP 3.5%	* An annual balance of the state debt in foreign trade cannot exist * A debt balance in foreign trade can exist only on single monthly levels

APPENDIX

A Brief Review of the Research Topics

1. Problems of Debts

Most highly developed countries of the world have problems with their debts. The first problem is that debts are too big from an economic aspect and are steadily increasing. Debts are generated from the base of foreign trade and the growth of state budget expenditures. Such economic moves are deviant.

2. Amortization of the Debts

The big problem is also that the states now have no economic ability to regularly amortize the debt. Amortizing means to reduce their size by a mathematical credit procedure. Let's take the example of the growth of U.S. debt. From 2000-13 the debt rose by more than three times, or at an average annual rate of around 23.3 percent. At the same time, the gross national product grew at an average rate about ten times less. Many other developed countries have similar situations. If the problem is approached from the postulate that a country can only spend what was produced then the conclusion is unmistakable. For the last thirteen years the United States has spent a lot more than they produced.

3. Debt Deviations

The debts of the debtor countries produce two economic deviations. First, a credit inversion is generated when the damage from the debt becomes greater than the benefits. Second, a state of eternal debt is created. This is a condition when the debt cannot be repaid within fifty years.

4. Danger of Economic Collapse

The emergence of credit inversion and eternal debt economic deviations creates the conditions for generating a third deviation, the breakdown of the entire economic system, an economic collapse. In this state, all normal levers of the state economic system lose strength. Economic activities collapse to a much lower level. All economic achievements are degraded. Out of these situations emerge undesirable social relations, fascism, communism, widespread poverty, and political revolutions.

5. Protection from the Economic Collapse

Protection from the economic collapse of the state is an important political issue. This is an area that should be dealt with by the political party in power, respecting the economic postulates. In this case, there are two basic theoretical tools: the principle of economic duals and the category of diversified money. Respecting the principles of economic duals, the concept of consuming only what is produced and to produce more efficiently is created. The introduction of the category of diversified money in foreign trade eliminates the deviation of generating an account deficit.

6. Characteristics of the Debt Situation

The current economic situation of the United States and of most developed countries is the state of credit inversion and the state of eternal debt. In addition, the mistake is often made of ignoring the notion of economic space. The result of this is an explicit economic deviation followed by an economic collapse.

7. The New Debt Situation

The new economic situation of the state presupposes the existence of economic security for the country as an economic space. This condition starts from the fact that politicians are the subjects of creating economic relations that are generated from the principle of economic duals and the category of diversified money. The substance of this condition presupposes an intra-state economic rationality and foreign trade balance. These principles do not allow politicians to advocate and promote national economic irrationality, spending over economic opportunities, unreasonableness in spending, deviance in economic relations, and preferring an economic policy that increases the stratification of society.

8. Final Comments of Research

The debts of nearly fifty countries around the world are too big and need to be several times lower. This can be achieved by savings in the state budget and taking advantage of the economic opportunities provided by the concept of economic duals. In foreign trade this can be achieved by introducing the application of the category of diversified money. Politics should not enter into the economics of state economic anomalies.

9. Criteria for Solving the Problem

In 1971, Richard Nixon abolished the Gold Standard and the convertibility of the dollar into gold. After that, money was able to be issued in unlimited amounts. Money was issued as credit debts. From that time, a stampede of money and debts began to develop.

Because of the above reasons, a scheme for the gradual recovery of the credit deviations on state levels is proposed. The scheme for the gradual recovery of debts of the state has six criteria. The state politicians will be fully responsible for this recovery.

List of Tables

List of Schemes

List of Figures

List of Examples

Bibliography

Books

Baletic, Z. *Ekonomski leksikon*, Leksikografski zavod 'Miroslav Krleza' i Masmedija, Zagreb 1995.

Belic M. et al., *EU Fondovi*, Novum, Zagreb 2008.

Cicin, Sain A. *Nekretnine potapaju burze*, Zivot s mirovinom broj 32, Zagreb 2008.

Canfield, J. *Nacela uspjeha*, Mozaik knjiga, Zagreb 2009.

Erega, S. *Sto banke ne zele da znate*, Profil, Zagreb 2009.

Ferguson, N. *Uspon novca – financijska povijest svijeta*, Naklada Ljevak d.o.o., Zagreb 2009.

Focic, G. and Novota, S. *Uokvirite svoju ideju, Prirucnik o upravljanju projektnim ciklusom i izradilogickog okvira*, Udruga za razvoj civilnog drustva SMART, Rijeka 2005.

Galbraith, J.K. Veliki slom 1929., V.B.Z. d.o.o., Zagreb 2010.

Krugman, P.R. and Obstfeld, M. *Međunarodna ekonomija*, Mate d.o.o., Zagreb 2010.

Napoleoni, C. *Ekonomska misao dvadesetog stoljeca*, Centar za kulturnu djelatnost, Zagreb 1982.

Obama, B. *Odvaznost nade - Razmišljanja o obnavljanju americkog sna*, Profil, Zagreb 2008.

Ovcaricek-Rostok, I. *The Economic Success of a State: The Principle of Economic Duals and Category of Diversified Money*, Strategic Book Publishing and Rights Co., Houston 2013.

Perisin, I. *Svjetski financijski vrtlog*, INTRO "Naprijed," Zagreb 1988.

Soldo, S. Financijske tablice, Narodne novine, Zagreb 1980.

Srića, V. *Hrvatska 2020 - jedina moguća budućnost*, Profil, Zagreb 2010.

Tehnicka enciklopedija 10 *Oru-Polj*, Jugoslavenski leksikografski zavod "Miroslav Krleza," Zagreb MCMXXXVI.

Tehnicka enciklopedija 12 *Sat-Teo*, Leksikografski zavod "Miroslav Krleza," Zagreb MCMXCII.

Tomljanovic, P. *Leksikon drzava svijeta*, Extrade, Rijeka 2005.

Van Doren, Charles. *Povijest znanja, proslost, sadasnjost i buducnost*, Mozaik knjiga, Zagreb 2005.

Von Neuman, J. and Morgenstern, O. *Theory of Games and Economic Behavior*, Princeton University Press, Princeton 1953

Official media

Framework Loan Agreement between Council of Europe Development Bank and the Republic of Croatia, Narodne novine 9/2007, Zagreb.

INDEX OF DATA SOURCES

Economic data for the U.S.: Wikipedia, http://www.wikipedia.org

Economic data for UK: Wikipedia, http://www.wikipedia.org

Economic data for Croatia: Wikipedia, http://www.wikipedia.org

Statisticki ljetopis 2003, Republika Hrvatska – Drzavni zavod za statistiku.

Statisticki ljetopis 2004, Republika Hrvatska – Drzavni zavod za statistiku.

Statisticki ljetopis 2005, Republika Hrvatska – Drzavni zavod za statistiku.

Statisticki ljetopis 2006, Republika Hrvatska – Drzavni zavod za statistiku.

Statisticki ljetopis 2007, Republika Hrvatska – Drzavni zavod za statistiku.

Statisticki ljetopis 2008, Republika Hrvatska – Drzavni zavod za statistiku.

Statisticki ljetopis 2009, Republika Hrvatska – Drzavni zavod za statistiku.

Statisticki ljetopis 2010, Republika Hrvatska – Drzavni zavod za statistiku.

Review Requested:

If you loved this book, would you please provide a review at Amazon.com?